ENGLISH LITERATURE

VOICES OF INDIAN DIASPORA

ENGLISH LITERATURE

VOICES OF INDIAN DIASPORA

Edited by

Malti Agarwal

ATLANTIC

PUBLISHERS & DISTRIBUTORS (P) LTD

Published by

ATLANTIC

PUBLISHERS & DISTRIBUTORS (P) LTD

7/22, Ansari Road, Darya Ganj,
New Delhi-110002
Phones : +91-11-40775252, 23273880, 23275880, 23280451
Fax : +91-11-23285873
Web : www.atlanticbooks.com
E-mail : orders@atlanticbooks.com

Branch Office
5, Nallathambi Street, Wallajah Road,
Chennai-600002
Phones : +91-44-64611085, 32413319
E-mail : chennai@atlanticbooks.com

Printed in India at Glorious Printers, A-13, D.S.I.D.C.,
Jhilmil Industrial Area, Delhi-110095

Preface

Diaspora is an emerging word in literature. Literature produced by the diasporic writers explores the problems and possibilities engendered by the experience of migrancy and diasporic life. Needless to say, it is gaining tremendous popularity among the lovers of literature.

The word 'diaspora', derived from the Greek word *diaspeiro*, literally means scattering or dispersion of the people from their homeland. It was first used by the Greeks for the movements of the Jews away from their homeland. Today, the term is applied to a number of ethnic and racial groups, living in an alien land.

People today are migrating to different parts of the world for one reason or the other. From India too, millions of people have migrated to various alien lands under 'forced exiles' or 'self-imposed exiles'. Some of them have made a mark in the field of writing. These immigrant writers reflect, on the one hand, their attachment to the motherland and on the other, their feeling of alienation and rootlessness. They suffer from psychic trauma and haunting presence of their lost homeland—the land of their birth—and also suffer from the anguish of reinventing home in the land of their choice.

The diasporic writings which are also known as 'expatriate writings' or 'immigrant writings' largely give voice to the traumatic experiences of the writers when they are on the rack owing to the clash of two cultures or the racial discrimination they undergo. Immigration proves a pleasant experience only to a few immigrants who succeed in assimilating themselves with new geographical, cultural, social and psychological environment. To most of the diasporic writers, immigration is not a delectable experience. They often find themselves sandwiched between two cultures. The feeling of nostalgia, a sense of loss and anxiety to reinvent home obsess them which find expression, consciously or unconsciously, in their writings. There are many diasporic writers, scattered in various countries like Britain, America, Canada, Australia, Malaysia, Mauritius, East Africa, Fiji, Trinidad and Tobago and so on. The writers like V.S. Naipaul, Vikram Seth, Rohinton Mistry, Uma Parameswaran, Salman Rushdie, Lakshmi Gill, Yasmin Gooneratne, and many others have left their country and settled abroad.

The present volume consists of twenty-two research papers, based on the works of the authors living in Canada, Australia and America. Indian diaspora has global presence. There are more than 20 million people of Indian origin, spread in 136 countries. They want their children to adopt Indian values. The works of all those among the Indian diaspora who have taken to writing exhibit their faith in hereditary cultural values. Most of the papers in this anthology are on such Indian writers who left their homeland either for earning livelihood or in pursuit of higher knowledge. The papers in this anthology study various issues relating to immigration like acculturation, multiculturation, transformation and marginalization which are reflected through the experiences of the protagonists during the course of assimilation in alien land.

The first two articles included in this volume cover the theoretical aspect of the diasporic literature. They also provide a historical and critical preview of the diasporic writers whether they are from India, Sri Lanka or from any other part of the world. A.N. Dwivedi's paper "Diasporic Writings in English" highlights the features of the diasporic literature, especially the literature of the Indian diaspora. Shrawan K. Sharma in his article "The World of Diasporic Poetry in Canada" discusses the distinct features of the diasporic poetry in Canada. Likewise, Samina Khan in her paper "Cultural Discordance: A Study of

Diasporic Writers in Canada" studies the theme of cultural discordance in the diasporic writings in Canada.

Among the Indian diaspora, Bharati Mukherjee occupies a distinctive place since she redefines the concept of diaspora. To most of the diasporic writers, immigration is synonymous with 'unhousement' and 'rootlessness', but to her it involves a process of gain. Her characters, in long as well as in short fiction, are set against divergent ethnic and cultural background. Though they encounter cultural crisis yet they soon explore new ways of 'belonging' and 'becoming' in the country of their choice. O.P. Budholia in his paper offers a peep into the extent of acculturation when he compares Bharati Mukherjee's *Jasmine* to Anita Desai's *Journey to Ithaca*. The papers by Beena Agarwal, Hemalatha K., Abha Shukla Kaushik, Ram Sharma and Archana Trivedi study various concerns in Bharati Mukherjee's novels.

Jhumpa Lahiri is a well-known name among the Indian diaspora of second generation. Next two articles throw light on the distinctiveness of two cultures which often traps her characters as shown in *Interpreter of Maladies*. Rohinton Mistry, who won the Governor General Award for fiction, left India for Canada. His books, like other diasporic writings, are concerned with "how the self is represented, seen and remembered against the backdrop of the past". My own paper studies Mistry's novel *Family Matters* as a diasporic text, whereas the article by J.P. Savita dwells on Mistry's short stories.

The book includes articles on the emerging writers of diaspora. Articles contributed by K.A. Agarwal, T.S. Anand and Sangeeta Das are attempts to highlight the works of the budding diasporic writers. The next two papers, authored by Beena Agarwal and Shalini Gupta, provide a close analysis of Chitra Banerjee Divakaruni's two story collections—*The Unknown Errors of Our Lives* and *Arranged Marriage*. A volume on the diasporic literature remains incomplete unless it refers to the works of Kiran Desai, the youngest winner of the prestigious Booker Prize and daughter of universally acclaimed Indian novelist, Anita Desai. The article on her novel, *The Inheritance of Loss,* is an attempt to assess if the author is another NRI writer obsessed by the themes like dislocation.

Among the older generation of the Indian diaspora, A.K. Ramanujan and Uma Parameswaran are the stalwarts. Neeta in her paper on Ramanujan analyses the nature of his poetry whereas Anuradha Verma studies Uma Parameswaran's story *The Door I Shut Behind Me* as a diasporic text.

Vikram Seth has emerged as a literary icon and is known all over the world for his unique technique and style. Malti Sharma in her article examines the fictional works of Vikram Seth and opines that human bonds—as strong as a rope of steel and as soft as a sigh—have been the foundation of his fictional works.

I thank all the contributors who have enriched this anthology with their well-researched articles. The book will be highly useful to the teachers and students of English Literature in various Indian universities, as well as to the researchers, particularly those working in the field of Indian diasporic literature.

Malti Agarwal

Contents

Diasporic Writings in English

1

A.N. Dwivedi

The term 'diaspora' (Greek in origin, derived from 'diaspeiro') literally means a scattering or dispersion of a group of people to an alien land, away from their traditional homelands. In olden days, the term was used for the worldwide scattering of the Jews outside Palestine. Now-a-days, it is applied to "a number of ethnic and racial groups" (McLeod *Preface* ix) living abroad.

We are mainly concerned, at the moment, with the writings of the Indian diaspora in English. Such writings are also known as 'expatriate writings' or 'immigrant writings'. The diasporic writings are generally marked by a sense of isolation and far-removedness from the mother-country. Hence such words as immigrant, exile and refugee are also applied to this brand of writing. 'Immigrant' indicates a location, a foreign settlement, and a physical movement, while 'exile' evokes "a variety of relationships with the mother-country—alienation, forced exile, self-imposed exile, political exile and so on" (Jain 12). The word 'refugee' denotes a person taking refuge in a foreign land for safety or for self-fulfilment. The diasporic writings combine all these features and attitudes in their texture.

The aesthetic of 'diaspora' emanates from the colonial experience of the people of the subject nation who, for want of opportunities of employment at home or due to exploitation by the colonizer, shift to another country. The immigrants, not necessarily indentured labourers, exercise a great impact on the culture, society and history of that country. At the same time, they nostalgically recall their motherland—its custom, culture, language and people—and creatively use these things in their writings if they are gifted intellectuals.

The main theorists of Diaspora are Edward Said, Gayatri Chakravorty Spivak and Homi Bhabha. These theorists are also the exponents of 'Colonialism' and 'Postcolonialism'. But while 'Colonialism/Postcolonialism' refer to the political and historical aspects of a country, the Diasporic theory is more preoccupied with the question of centrality, hybridity, ambience, transculturation of the people. Diasporic writing is concerned with what Edward Said calls "not only of a basic geographical distinction but also a whole sense of 'interests'" (12). Edward Said's *Orientalism* (1978) envisages the Orient as 'the Other' that is dominated by the Occident in the power-game. This naturally allots 'an inferior status' to the 'subject-races', and the sense of inferiority, insecurity, joblessness, or the dream of better prospect outside is the cause of the dispersion of the Diaspora. Edward Said's theory that "knowledge gives power, more power requires more knowledge, and so on in an increasingly profitable dialectic of information and control" (36) corroborates this idea. Gayatri Spivak, who convincingly evolves the notion of 'subalternity', also believes that 'the Third World' (Said's 'the Other World') is a creation of the West which distorts, even resorts to violence towards the non-Western cultures. Spivak's theory of 'subalternity' (*i.e.,* being of lower status) encompasses women, blacks, the colonized and the working class. Her famous essay "Can the Subaltern Speak?"(Spivak) mainly addresses itself to the 'muteness' of women in postcolonial societies. In contrast to Said's emphatic assertion of 'identity' or 'centrality' that an exile or expatriate should seek in order to save himself/herself, Homi Bhabha upholds the tenet of 'hybridity' in the cultural context, and his poetics of 'disjunctive temporality', which is analogous to Salman Rushdie's notion of 'broken mirror' about the immigrant, makes a 'mimicry' of the notion of 'centrality'. Bhabha's temporality "creates a signifying time for the inscription of cultural incommensurability" (177).

The diasporic writings in English are evidently produced by persons of Indian origin who are presently living outside their country. The diasporic writers are now scattered throughout the world, and are found in such diverse places as Fiji, Trinidad, and Guyana (where they are in minority), and in Malaysia, Mauritius and East Africa, and in Western countries like Britain, America, Canada and Australia.

Right from the dawn of Indian Writing in English, the talented Indians have been going abroad and reaping a rich literary harvest out of a commingling of cultures and languages. Prof. K.R. Srinivasa Iyengar in his book, *Indian Writing in English* (1962), thinks that "modern Indian literature" begins with Raja Rammohan Roy (1774-1833), who "was destined to act as a bridge between India and England," (30) and we know that Roy was a master of English prose. The Dutts and the Ghoses frequently shuttled between Europe and India. Who does not know the life-history of Michael Madhusudan Dutt, Toru Dutt, Romesh Chander Dutt, Manmohan Ghose, and Sri Aurobindo? They all were born Indians, but shifted to the West for academic and literary pursuits. In due course, they produced works of lasting value. Madhusudan's *Meghnad Badha* (which was rendered in English in 1879), Toru's *Ancient Ballads* (1882) and her earlier book of translations *A Sheaf Gleaned in French Fields* (1876), Romesh Chunder's skilled translations of *Sansar* (*The Lake of Palms,* 1902) and *Madhvi Kankan* (*The Slave Girl of Agra,* 1909), Manmohan's *Love Songs and Elegies* (1898), and Sri Aurobindo's *Savitri* (1950-51) are some of the outstanding works by all means. The award of the Nobel Prize in literature to Thakur Rabindranath Tagore for his *Gitanjali* in 1913 stimulated a number of authors to write in English. Sarojini Naidu, M.K. Gandhi, Jawaharlal Nehru, Mulk Raj Anand, R.K. Narayan, Raja Rao and a host of other authors expressed themselves in English with ease and command. But all these authors returned to India after their short or a little long stay in the West.

The diasporic writing proper has, however, a worldwide context; and it includes writers of both old and new generations who have left India and settled abroad. Of the old generation of such writers, we may mention Kamala Markandaya, B. Rajan, Santha Rama Rau, Bharati Mukherjee, Anita Desai, Salman Rushdie, Vikram Seth, V.S. Naipaul, Nirad Chaudhari, Amitav Ghosh, Ved Mehta and A.K. Ramanujan.

Kamala Markandaya, who was married to Mr. Taylor and who might be called "the fourth wheel" (Dwivedi 10) of Indian English Novel, has been a prolific writer, with ten novels to her credit. Many of her novels deal with the theme of East-West encounter, and in them the characters are drawn from both India and England. We come across in them 'nostalgic longings for India'—one of the salient features of the diasporic writing. Markandaya's novels—*Some Inner Fury* (1955), *Possession* (1963), *The Coffer Dams* (1969), *The Nowhere Man* (1972), *The Golden Honeycomb* (1977), and *Pleasure City* (1982) are to be marked in this connection.

B. Rajan, who is more known as a literary critic of Milton, Yeats and Eliot, than as a creative writer, has published two novels, *The Dark Dancer* (1958) and *Too Long in the West* (1961). Like his protagonist Krishnan in *The Dark Dancer,* B. Rajan has lived too long in the West—in England, America and Canada. Presently he is settled in Toronto (Canada). Here his daughter, Tilottama Rajan must be mentioned as an authoress of *Myth in a Metal Mirror* (1967), which is a poetical collection containing 36 poems in all, though she belongs to the younger generation of diasporic writers.

Santha Rama Rau (whose full name is Vasanthi Rama Rau Bowers) was educated in England and America and was married to an American. She is now settled in America, and has authored such books as *Home to India* (1945), *Remember the House* (1956), and *Gifts of Passage* (1961), and *The Adventures* (1971). Very often she is not considered an Indian writer, reminding us of the case of Bharati Mukherjee, and yet Prof. S.K. Desai in his critical book on this author argues that Rau "has essentially an Indian identity" (10). Rau is well known for her scripting of the dramatic version of E.M. Forster's *A Passage to India.*

Bharati Mukherjee comes close on the heels of Santha Rama Rau. Though she, like Markandaya, retains her maiden name, she is much more westernized or better Americanized. She has written six novels like *The Tiger's Daughter*, *Wife*, *Jasmine, Leave It To Me, The Holder of the World* and *Desirable Daughters.* She represents the Indian woman in a cross-cultural context. She is out to seek a new identity for herself, but it turns out to be a broken identity. The female protagonists of Mukherjee's novels usually suffer from a sense of frustration and loneliness (for example, Dimple Dasgupta in *Wife).* Mukherjee collaborated with her husband, Clark Blaise, in writing a novel, *Days and Nights in Calcutta* (1977), which is actually "an autobiographical summation of her [Mukherjee's] return to her country after fourteen years of absence in North America" (Sunitha 263).

Anita Desai has, of late, become a diasporic writer of eminence. Earlier when she was in residence at New Delhi, she produced about a dozen novels mainly portraying the abnormal and hypersensitive women in untoward situations. Her novels like *Cry, The Peacock* (1963), *Voices in the City* (1965), *Bye-Bye, Blackbird* (1971), and *Fire on the Mountain* (1977) are to be specially marked in this connection. One of Anita's frequently used subjects is cross-cultural contact between the East and the West and the resultant sense of alienation and frustration in her dominant characters. It must be mentioned here that her daughter, Kiran Desai (born 1971), is also a diasporic writer with two novels to her credit, *Hullabaloo under the Guava Orchard* (1999) and *The Inheritance of Loss* (2006).

Salman Rushdie is pre-eminently concerned with the treatment of history and religion. His *Midnight's Children* (1980) ushers in a new era of fictional art; it is a postmodern novel which reveals "the unreliability of historical discourse" (Lindsay 170). In this novel, the protagonist Saleem Sinai is presented as a troubled and fragmented soul. He suffers from a sense of identity crisis, and the harrowing tale of Mother India during the days of partition becomes his own. Rushdie's novel, *Shame* (1983), portrays the troubled and violent political situation in Pakistan. His *Satanic Verses* (1988) is a novel that has stirred a hornet's nest and has been banned in many Muslim countries, even in India, Pakistan and South Africa.

Vikram Seth is a stupendous diasporic writer who has demonstrated his expertise in both prose and poetry. He began with prose and then shifted to poetry. His travel book, *From Heaven Lake,* and poetical collection entitled *The Humble*

Administrator's Garden both appeared in 1983, followed by *The Golden Gate* (1986), *All You Who Sleep Tonight* (1990), and *Beastly Tales from Here and There* (1992), and *A Suitable Boy* (1993). If *The Golden Gate* is a *tour de force* in poetic form, *A Suitable Boy* is one of the longest novels in world literature. It runs into nearly fourteen hundred pages and has earned for Seth the title of "a new Tolstoy" (Pathak 70). Seth draws upon his rich Indian experience in writing this novel (which is set in the land of his birth).

V.S. Naipaul, the winner of the Nobel Prize for literature in 2001, tries in his writings to revive his connections with the past. He is separated from India by two generations—it was his grandfather who had left India for Trinidad. From the West Indies Naipaul shifted to England for his residence. Thus, he is "sufficiently removed in both time and space" (Huggan 136) from India. His three travel books—*An Area of Darkness* (1964), *India: A Wounded Civilization* (1977), and *India: A Million Mutinies* (1991)—are directly based on his visits to India and on his perceptions and experiences there. In them as also in his novels there is an acute sense of anxiety born of displacement. Naipaul remarks in his novel *A House for Mr. Biswas* (1961) thus: "Mr. Biswas found it easy to imagine the other race of Indians moving about this road before the world grew dark for them" (397).

Like Naipaul, Nirad Chaudhuri is also critical of and apathetic towards India. Based in London, Chaudhuri burst upon the Indian literary scene with the publication of *The Autobiography of an Unknown Indian* (1951). But more than a personal history, it is a national history in a distorted colour. Whether one agrees with his views on Indian history and civilization is a different matter, but he is "probably India's finest living writer of English prose" (Harrex 22). Apparently, he suffers from a colonial hang-over and shows extra-fidelity towards the erstwhile masters of India. This attitude of his persists in his other works too—*A Passage to England* (1959), *The Continent of Circé* (1966), *To Live or Not to Live* (1971), etc.

Amitav Ghosh has also lived long in England, Egypt and America. For him, globalization (or, moving across the national frontiers) is "an everyday fact of existence" (Thieme 274). He seems to believe in *The Shadow Lines* (1988) that the national boundaries are merely 'political fictions'. The two other novels of importance written by him are: *The Circle of Reason* (1986) and *The Calcutta Chromosome* (1996). In his novels Amitav remains a wandering internationalist, disowning the theory of cultural centrality—that 'a culture is rooted in a single place'.

Ved Mehta (born 1934) is a notable diasporic writer who migrated to the U.S.A. from Bombay. He became blind at the age of three, and yet he writes with an acute sense of reality around him. If his autobiography, *Face to Face* (1957), brings out his perceptions and experiences of life, in most of his other prose works he projects the image of India and her people, their customs and rituals, in an absorbing manner. He nostalgically recalls his past associations with Mother India, with his relatives and friends in such works as *The New India* (1978), *Mamaji* (1979), *The Photographs of Chachaji* (1982 etc.).

Of all the Indian English poets, A.K. Ramanujan (1929-93) occupies a place of pride. Since the very beginning of the Sixties, he had been living in the U.S.A., where he was a Professor of Linguistics at the University of Chicago. In his lifetime he had published three volumes of poetry—*The Striders* (1966), *Relations* (1971), and *Second Sight* (1986). His fourth volume appeared posthumously in 1995 under the caption, *The Black Hen.* Ramanujan has also produced some laudable works of translation (e.g., *The Interior Landscape,* 1967; *Speaking of Siva,* 1972; *Samskara,* 1976; *Poems of Love and War,* 1985; etc.). Recalling his days in India, Ramanujan remarks as follows: "But living/ among relations/ binds the feet." (*Relations,* n.p.). Speaking highly of him, Susanne and Lloyd Rudolph have commented thus: "A polymath; a demanding scholar with demanding standards; a teller of tales, a mesmerizing poet" (8).

The above survey of the old generation of diasporic writers leads us to believe that they have lived long or 'too long' in the West and that they are generally scattered in the whole world—in England, America, Canada and West Indies in particular. The countrywide distribution or dispersion of the writers of Indian diaspora is as follows: Kamala Markandaya, Anita Desai, Salman Rushdie, Vikram Seth, Amitav Ghosh are Britain-based. Even V.S. Naipaul is presently settled in England; he is a twice-removed author who has shifted to England from Trinidad (West Indies). Similarly, B. Rajan has migrated to Canada from England, and in both the places he worked as Professor of English. Santha Rama Rau and Bharati Mukherjee have been living in the United States of America.

After England, Canada has immensely attracted the diasporic writers. Since long Saros Cowasjee has taken his residence in Canada. He published his novel, *Goodbye to Elsa,* in 1974, and in it the protagonist Tristan, the one-eyed man, runs away from his heavyweight wife, Elsa Harbour (of 180 pounds), and one-year old son. He gets entangled with diverse women like Jane, Lydia, Heather Malleson, Marie and Marion, and in a mood of frustration tries to kill himself, bidding 'goodbye' to his wife. Cowasjee makes some witty remarks about persons and places in this novel. Thus, he once makes Tristan to observe: "Besides, the Canadians are so neutral: they are neither sane nor insane, good nor bad. They generally take the colour from their surroundings" (*Goodbye to Elsa* 142). The writer shows his concern here for the sovereign nationality and identity of Canada: "We have to be on the guard all the time against the Americanisation of Canada. It is a matter of preserving our Canadian identity" (117).

Like Cowasjee, Cyril Dabydeen is an old settler in Canada. He is also twice-removed geographically; his grandfather, an indentured labourer, had moved from India to Guyana (West Indies), where this author was born, and in 1970 he [Cyril] shifted from Guyana to Canada. He is "one of the most prolific writers" (McLeod 189) being both poet and novelist. He has about 20 books to his credit. *Poems in Recession* (1972) is his first volume of poems, and it was followed by *Goatsong* (1977), *Heart's Frame* (1979), *Dark Swirl* (1988), *Coastland* (1989—all poetical collections), and *Still Close to the Islands* (1980), *To Monkey Jungle* (1988), *The Wizard Swami* (1985 and 1989), *Berbice Crossing* (1996), and *Black Jesus & Other Stories*

(1996—all story-books). Cyril Dabydeen has paid visits to India, first time in 1987.

Other diasporic writers who have gone over to Canada and settled there are of relatively younger generation. Besides Tilottama Rajan who has already been referred to, Uma Parameswaran, Ashish Gupta, Rohinton Mistry, Neil Bissoondath, and M.G. Vassanji, are to be mentioned in this connection. Of these writers, Uma Parameswaran is a Professor of English at the University of Winnipeg, and she has done some commendable creative work. She burst on the literary scene with her book of poems, *Cyclic Hope Cyclic Pain,* in 1973. The volume consists of barely nine poems and a dance-drama entitled "Meera". Poems are simply numbered (no title is given), and "Meera" contains five short scenes related to the life of Meera, who is portrayed here as "a handmaid of Lord Krishna now and forever" (Parameswaran 15). Uma has also written another dance-drama called *Sita's Promise* (1981) wherein Sita is depicted as delicate and childlike. Rama suspects her ability to be the Queen of Ayodhya, but Lakshman defends her and even blames Rama for neglecting the call of love for the sake of duty. The portrayal of these characters in a new light shows Uma Parameswaran's "expatriate sensibility" that has effected "a dynamic act of remythologisation" (James 203). Parameswaran has also written *Trishanku* (1987), a series of monologues spoken by various personae, highlighting a sense of alienation, rootlessness and nostalgia in the lives of Savitri Bhave and her husband Sharad, who hail from Ahmedabad and are now settled in Canada. The book of poems, however, ends on a note of reconciliation between the wife and the husband, signalling a tension-free future for their children.

Ashish Gupta, who went to America and then to Canada from Patna, has made a mark in diasporic writing with his two novels, *Dying Traditions* (1992) and *The Toymaker from Wiesbaden* (1993). Rohinton Mistry is another such writer of power and pulse, having published remarkable works like *Tales from Ferozshah Baag* (1987), *Such a Long Journey* (1991), *A Fine Balance* (1996) and *Family Matters* (2002). An East Indian who migrated to Canada from the Caribbean, Neil Bissoondath claims to be a 'Canadian Writer'. He has published two collections of short stories, *Digging Up the Mountain* (1985) and *On the Eve of Uncertain Tomorrows* (1990), and two novels, *A Casual Brutality* (1988) and *The Innocence of Age* (1992). Also, M.G. Vassanji has created ripples in the literary world by his modernistic work, *No New Land* (1992), and experimental novel, *The Book of Secrets* (1995).

Two of the younger diasporic writers based in Britain are: Pico Iyer and Gita Mehta. Iyer's parents had shifted to London from Bombay, and Iyer was born in Oxford in 1957. Iyer keeps moving from England to Japan and to Cuba, as a result of which he produced two travelogues, a memoir set in Japan, *The Lady and the Monk* (1991), and a novel located in Cuba, *Cuba and the Night* (1995), and numerous essays. As for Gita Mehta, she has shot into fame with her novel, *A River Sutra* (1993), where the journey motif is so dominant. Mehta's novel is comparable to Kipling's *Kim* (1901) for employing the theme of search for a mythic river.

The U.S.A. houses Chitra Bannerjee Divakaruni, Meena Alexander and Jhumpa Lahiri as diasporic writers of younger generation. Chitra has produced *The Mistress of Spices* (1997), which is a story of Tilo, and Meena has published three books of poetry from W.W. and a memoir called *Fault Lines* (1993). Jhumpa Lahiri has become so popular with her first collection of short stories, *Interpreter of Maladies* (1999), which won for her the coveted Pulitzer Prize in 2000. In this matter, Lahiri is comparable to Arundhati Roy who bagged the Booker Prize for her novel, *The God of Small Things* (1997). The blurb describes Lahiri's book containing nine stories *in toto* thus: "Jhumpa Lahiri's elegant stories tell the lives of Indians in exile, of people navigating between the strict traditions they've inherited and the baffling New World they must encounter every day." (Qtd. from the blurb).

By now, two dozens of important diasporic writers have been mentioned. Here two more writers who deserve to be mentioned are Sujata Bhatt, who is living in Germany, and Mena Abdullah, who is a Punjabi migrant to Australia. Sujata and Mena represent the Indian diaspora focusing on the disturbing sense of dislocation in their writings. Their expatriate sensibility is effectively expressed in what Meena Alexander calls "a shifting frame of reference, of multiple worlds", (Interview 3) which characterizes the postcolonial situation. Sujata's collection of poems entitled *Brunizem* (1988) and Mena's book of short stories, *Time of the Peacock* (1965—written with Ray Mathew) clearly reflect the 'shifting frame of reference'.

Finally, the above account of the diasporic writings in English convinces us that the Indian immigrants and expatriates have produced a rich harvest of literature in multiple forms and *genres,* in diverse attitudes and backgrounds. The diasporic writers are settled abroad in different countries—in Britain, Canada, America, Germany, Australia, and West Indies. They belong to both old and young generations. Their writings bring to the fore their awareness of geographical dislocation, cultural ambivalence, social and political alienation, and absence of centrality. Memory and nostalgia connect them with their homeland and past associations, which feed their imagination to churn out something 'new and strange'.

WORKS CITED

Alexander, Meena. "Freedom and the Indian Diaspora: An Interview." *The Hindu Literary Review*. Chennai, 21 December, 1997.

Bhabha, Homi. *The Location of Culture.* London and New York: Routledge, 1994.

Cowasjee, Saros. *Goodbye to Elsa.* London, Sydney and Toronto: The Bodley Head, 1974.

Desai, S.K. *Santha Rama Rau.* New Delhi: Arnold Heinemann, 1976.

Dwivedi, A.N. "Indian Fiction in English: Retrospect and Prospect." *Studies in Contemporary Indian Fiction in English.* Allahabad: Kitab Mahal, 1987.

Harrex, S.C. *The Fire and the Offering*, Vol. I. Calcutta: Writers Workshop, 1977.

Huggan, Graham. "Frustration and Fraudelence: V.S. Naipaul's India." *The Literature of the Indian Diaspora*, Ed. A.L. McLeod. New Delhi: Sterling Publishers Pvt. Ltd., 2000.

Iyengar, K.R. Srinivasa. *Indian Writing in English.* 4th revised and enlarged edition. New Delhi: Sterling Publishers Pvt. Ltd., 1984.

Jain, Jasbir. "Introduction." *Writers of the Indian Diaspora.* Jaipur and New Delhi: Rawat Publications, 1998.

James, Jancy. "Remythologizing as Expatriate Vision and Art: An Intertextual Reading of Uma Parameswaran's Sita's *Promise* and *Meera.*" *Writers of the Indian Diaspora.* Ed. Jasbir Jain, 1998.

Lahiri, Jhumpa. "Blurb." *Interpreter of Maladies.* New Delhi: Harper Collins Publishers India, 1999.

Lindsay, Allan. "Salman Rushdie, History, and the Contemporary Novel." *The Literature of the Indian Diaspora.* Ed. McLeod.

McLeod, A.L. "Preface." *The Literature of the Indian Diaspora.* New Delhi: Sterling Publishers Pvt. Ltd., 2000.

——. "Cyril Dabydeen: Remembrance of Things Indian." *The Literature of the Indian Diaspora*, 2000.

Naipaul, V.S. *A House for Mr. Biswas.* London: Andre Deutsch, 1961.

Parameswaran, Uma. *Cyclic Hope, Cyclic Pain.* Calcutta: Writers Workshop, 1973.

Pathak, R.S. Ed. Editorial, *Recent Indian Fiction*, New Delhi: Prestige Books, 1994.

Said, Edward. *Orientalism.* London: Routledge, 1978.

Spivak, Gayatri Chakravorty. "Can the Subaltern Speak?" *Marxism and the Interpretation of Culture.* Eds. Gay Nelson and Lawrence Grassberg. London: Macmillan, 1998.

Sunitha, K.T. "Cross-Cultural Dilemmas of Indian Women in Bharati Mukherjee's Fiction." *The Literature of the Indian Diaspora.* Ed. A.L. McLeod, 2000.

Susanne and Lloyd Rudolph. "Remembering Raman." *The Times of India*, 25 July 1993.

Thieme, John. "The Discoverer Discovered: Amitav Ghosh's *The Calcutta Chromosome.*" *The Literature of the Indian Diaspora.* Ed. McLeod, 2000.

The World of Diasporic Poetry in Canada

2

Shrawan K. Sharma

The diasporic writing has been receiving increasingly academic and disciplinary recognition throughout the globe. It has emerged into a distinct literary genre. Its emergence has produced a radical transformation or 'paradigm shift' in literary and cultural studies. It is in the process of acquiring canonical status. The diasporic writers are often concerned with giving a voice to the displaced and dislocated. More significantly, they are all determined to narrate, and thus put on record their pasts–bequeathed memories, oral testimonies, remembered histories and stories. Besides their response to the past, they do not spare any opportunity to versify their reaction to the alien land where they came as immigrants. Their nostalgic response to their homeland and reaction to the alien land lead to a kind of hope for change of the alien land into a new homeland. This account tells us that their background serves as the basis of their poetry upon which it flourishes. This background has two phases of their experience. The first phase consists of their cultural, religious, educational and experimental experiences of the homeland which they are already equipped with and which they are proud of and so make their inheritance a part of their writing. As far as the second phase is concerned, it is filled with their immediate experiences in the hostile, social environment where they feel themselves doubly marginalized: first they are immigrants and second because they belong to racial often linguistic, usually religious minorities. In a word, the alienation of the immigrant and the bitter stings of racism and religious bigotry, the painful daily realities and their native civilization and traditions are important factors in shaping their lives, politics and art. The present study is to articulate the diasporic journey and its experience in Canada as a constructive process of reconciliation with, affirmation and acceptance of space and stable values.

The central feature of the diasporic writing is a journey that starts from one's homeland to an alien land and then with a sense of loss in the hostile social environment, ceaselessly struggles and then at last with a hope of change starts the process of reconciliation, assimilation and affirmation. This is a journey from the centre to the periphery and again from the periphery to the centre. Needless to say that there are many variations upon this scene, and the one essential thing is that there should be three distinct regions. The regions which the diasporic poets themselves employ are the homeland, the alien land and the new homeland. The diasporic poets who have a straightforward exposition of this journey, identify these regions with the past, the present and the future and that is generally the case when the journey denotes the historic time. More frequently, however, it denotes the life of an immigrant, and then the three regions are the home culture, alien culture and the multiculture. Whichever they be, they invariably have the same character: the first is a period of joyous innocence when one lives in harmony with social and natural climate, the second is a period of suffering when one is alone in a hostile world, and the third is a period of reconciliation in which suffering subsides into a new hope for space.

The basis for this view is found in a conception of diaspora which has been widespread in different periods. It has been put forward in the entries on diaspora in dictionaries and encyclopedias by various scholars. There the term "diaspora' denotes a process by which people of particular nation become scattered in other countries. It has been a history-specific term as it has been referred to "the settlement abroad of the Jews, hummed out from their homeland by Nazi intolerance." The fundamental premise of this expulsion are:

— it is associated with the sense of displacement;

— it carries a sense of desire for the return to their roots;

— it has feeling of nostalgia and remembrance of the home country;
— it is associated with a sense of loss;
— it informs the diasporic consciousness;
— it involves a painful process of acculturation and adjustment.

In the modern context too, these features are very much relevant as the term denotes a dispersal or spreading of people originally belonging to one nation or having a common culture. This sense of displacement, desire for the return to their roots, feelings of nostalgia, remembrance of the homeland with a sense of loss that informs the diasporic consciousness and the experience of a painful process of acculturation and adjustment is common to all who have left their homeland for an alien land. At the end of his work *Culture and Imperialism,* Edward Said quotes a twelfth century monk from Saxony Hugo of St. Vicar where he elaborates his journey of the exile from his homeland to the globe. He holds that the exile first becomes 'tender' (who finds his homeland sweet), then 'strong' (to whom every soil is his native one) and finally 'perfect' (to whom the entire world is a foreign place) (44). The diasporic poets who find themselves sandwich between two cultures: "born under one law, to another bound" (Parameswaran 15) move from faith and joy through the center of indifference to the mature faith or understanding. This three-fold pattern arises from the alteration of vital or organic periods, which are periods of faith and imagination, with mechanical or critical periods, which are periods of skepticism dominated by the understanding. Thus the total pattern is always a three-fold cycle of thesis, antithesis and synthesis repeating itself over and over again. To the diasporic poets this cycle of three consists of the past, the present and the future which may be understood as feeling of nostalgia, sense of loss and consciousness of the new homeland.

Though we have called the experiences of the diasporic poets in Canada the three regions: the homeland, the alien land and new homeland, it should be understood that the symbols of diasporic poets take forms not actually denoted by these name.

The diasporic poets in Canada have for example warm land, the icy land and the glimmering of river. Respectively they also employ the flora and fauna and the customs and traditions of the homeland, the members of the family like grandmother, grandfather, mother, father, son, daughter, sister—all these denote the warm glade. The second region too has flora and fauna of the alien land, a place where people are struggling in a cold forbidding climate. For this region there is an important aspect, i.e. a ship symbolism which is quite distinct from his symbolism of icy land. Nonetheless, it has the same structure and conveys a similar meaning. It should not be confused with the sea of death into which the river of life flows. For their image of the sea is precisely comparable to the icy land which is a metaphor for alienation, struggle, terror and manifestation of inhuman void. And finally, parallel to the glimmering of river is an alternative symbol for the third phase of life which we may call the "igloo of heaven" (Gill *Revolution* 30).

The first region of the diasporic world is usually presented as a place of richness and warmth, a place of birth and ancestors where the persons who inhabit it live there free from the crisis of identity and untroubled by the sense of loss which later shakes them in the alien land, Canada. It is a place, Lakshmi Gill holds "where flowers bloom from navels/hot lands of my birth fall-fall into a full revolution" (Crusz *Homecomings* 90). Uma Parameswaran also considers this region full of love, glory and brightness. She holds that

> There was a time
> When words came to me
> And I strung them
>   as my grandmother strung glass beads
>   to curtain her doorways
>   tubes, spheroids and decahedrons,
>   red, sky blue, yellow and green. (13)

In these lines the lexical field is noteworthy to portray the feature of this region. Here the employment of the words "grandmother", "glass beads", and "curtain" evokes an aura of love. The use of colours "red", "skyblue" and "yellow" and "green" suggests that the life of this region is full of vigour and happiness. The man is in tune with his fellow beings and knows them well and pays "his rich ready response to their respectful salutations" (Parameswaran 16). There is also a celebration of pastoral and elemental simplicities and homespun emotional reality. In the poem *Trishanku,* Usha, an inhabitant of this region who

> ...was born in that magic hour
> when the unseen sun pierces arrows
> across the silver sky
> as sleep amorous Earth
> opens languorous arms
> against still-dreaming shadows. (Parameswaran 20)

and who stands for both morning and the female character is suggestive of the elemental simplicities, away from the trappings of civilization, leading a serene life far away from the madding crowd and ignoble strife. Surjeet Kalsey considers this region "filled with the honest voices,/ the soft touches", "confusing sounds of two/ passions: children and creativity." (I want my chaos back 57).

The icy land, the second region of the diasporic worlds is the very antithesis of the warm glade. Far from being a place where one is a part of the social fabric, it is likely to be a place where one is all alone, alienated and is struggling for ones identity. Where the first was a protected place, the second is precariously open, exposed, frozen arctic wasteland. It is at once terrifyingly full: the one thing that it is not harmoniously unified. "It scares [the inhabitant], this other world/ that intrudes on [him]/ of a sudden/ in everyday actions" (Parameswaran 69). It bears the sufferings, experienced in physical and social cold of the new country, i.e. Canada.

This region has oppositions that are central to the work of diasporic poets: oppositions between Canada and the homeland as places to live, between past and present heritage, between English language and homeland experience, between the homeland of memory and the reality of today—itself split between capitalist prosperity and spiritual, human suffering. Crusz's second collection, *Elephant and Ice* has probably been the most influential in foregrounding the duality through the images of "elephant" and "ice" and through the persona of the "sun-man", "winter-man" and "raven", all of which the poet assumes to be different facets of the migrant experience which serve as markers for relating the experience of living on the cusp of alienation, racism, identity and nostalgia. Crusz has courted this image with a substantial body of poems that move from one end of the spectrum of the migration to the other, celebrating, critiquing, and ironizing these two worlds. In "Elegy for the Sun-Man's Children Going" he speaks of "This immigrant poet? whose road was never his, but went" (The Selected Poems 28) and in "Dark with Excessive Bright" he admits: "Dark I am/ and darkly do I sing" (The Selected Poems 90).

Here the first reaction is of anger. Even a casual reader can feel a violent but constructive anger that wells-up through their poetry. Their personal sense of marginalization makes them fiercely search out, relate to, and empathize with fellow sufferers. This sense of reaction so much a part of the immigrant psyche is very much pronounced in their poetry. Dionne Brand uses the trope of reaction to describe her relationship with Canada in her *untitled poem*:

> I am not a refugee
> I have my papers'
> I was born in the Caribbean
> Practically in the sea
> Fifteen degrees above the equator
> I have a Canadian passport
> I have lived here all my adult life
> I am stateless anyway. (63)

Looking around on the icy land, the persona is bitterly indignant that the world should be such a place and that all his dreams have been destroyed. In "Visual", a poem of *Trishanku,* we hear the angry voice of the narrator who asserts the rights of the immigrants, who have been living here for last three hundred years. He says: "Look you guys, we've gotta show them/ yeah, show the bastards we've as much/ right as anyone who has come here" and so advises the immigrants to "stand together, and they ain't gonna/ divide and rule/ no more" (Parameswaran 76).

In the process of exploring their predicament, the diasporic poets very often evoke Canadian ethos, its geography, its city space in order to juxtapose them against their home environment. Such juxtapositions in themselves are significant. This feature occurs in Crusz's poetry in the form of sensuous imagery of flowers, fruits and the beauty of nature in Sri Lanka, as against the cold, the snow and the bleakness of Canada. On the one hand, the sun-man remembers

> how he once lived;
> on a fistful of rice,
> shared of dried fish
> mango and pineapple,
> coconut milk dripping
> from his mouth.... (Elephant and Ice 20)

On the other, in an alien land, the sun-man crawls

> into his sun-dial nerve
> and sleeps
> with myths and shibboleths
> as central heating steals
> under his dark eyelids. (Elephant and Ice 35)

This shade of discord caused by oppositions in Crusz's poetry narrates the endlessly repeating history of his journey from Ceylon to Canada (1)—a retelling of the process of displacement. Uma Parameswaran versifies this nostalgia and exposes the sad facade that it actually is. Despite the fact that life is luxurious, the mother, in one of her poems, feels imprisoned and so says:

> I am too used to the sounds
> Of living things
> Of birds in the morning
> Of rain and wind at night
> Not the drone of furnace fan
> And hiss of hot blasts
> And hose of washing machine
> Open the windows, son,
> And let me go back

To sun and air
And sweat and even flies and all
But not this, not this. (62)

This region also includes cultural rootlessnesss felt by the immigrants and diasporic poets. In Uma Parameswaran's *Trishanku*, a mythical figure, a king who floats between heaven and earth, rejected by both, is a useful metaphor for displaced people. In the poem there are sixteen figures—poet, Chander, Usha, Chandrika, Dilip, Sharad, Savitri, Jayanta, Bihari, Poornima, Tara, Suri, Tara's Mother-in-law, Veejala, Visual, and Vithal—to express nostalgic pain and Canadian consciousness. The following utterance exemplifies this rootlessness caused by the nostalgic feelings and Canadian consciousness:

We are new Canadians
Come from many races
Black, White, Olive brown
All alike, for all the many places
High tech, mid tech or no tech
Are one.
What we were not told, never told, never guessed,
It is written in our children's faces
Furrowed with tears because of our race
Or colour or tongue that stumbles
Over words so alien to the many places
From which we have come
Will doors shut on them as on us?
Landlord's, employer's, neighbour's?
Have come from Niger and Luzon
From the Antilles and Hongkong
To these vast spaces
Only to see our young ones' faces
Slapped by unthinking scorn
Unfeeling barbs
From closed fists and closed heart? (15)

The poet is agonized to find herself in the state of *trishanku* as "born under one law, to another bound" (15) and so she feels bewildered:

And what shall I do now, Fulke Greville
And What?
Shall I hand myself in the sky
As Trishanku did of old?
What new elect shall I lead
To what Sinai to bring down
What law? (15)

This state of *trishanku* also finds expression in *Migratory Birds* of Surjeet Kalsey. On the one hand, she seems to be confident to go back to the homeland while on the other she also realizes some force which checks her return from the alien land to the homeland:

We
the migratory birds
are here this season
thinking
we will fly
back to our home
for sure. (40)

But

No one knows
which invisible cage imprisons us?
and the flight begins to die slowly
in our wings.
Some of us are drawn with
the chain
some lag
in the swamp
no sun, no earth
where to look at, what to look for? (40)

Himani Bannerji's title poem of the collection, *Doing Time* depicts Canada as a prison house for those who are "not white" (9). This sense of reaction and alienation, a part of the immigrant psyche, is very often contrasted with the nostalgic reminiscences of the world left behind. Laksmi Gill's poem "Revolution" interfuses Canada the cold alien land with the warm tropical homeland:

...this arid country
stretching from the stretch marks
of my belly to beyond my reach
rippled cracks, pattern of dead
photographed images, untitled lines
that fall from edge to other
universes I dream of—there
where flowers bloom from navels
hot lands of my birth—fall
into a full revolution. It's time
isn't it time to go? O soil, turn over. (30)

The poem is conceptualized in terms of death and barrenness, giving way to birth and creation, couched appropriately, in images of the earth. The same feature is discernible in the poem, "Paki Go Home" of Himani Bannerji. The poet expresses her indignation against the dominant group of whites and finally seeks the dissolution of her discords in a psychological and philosophical stance on her sense of oneness. The first stanza shows the harsh attitude shown to and the violence inflicted by Canadian on the immigrants "cut at the knees, hands chopped, eyes blinded/ mouth stopped, voices lost" (5). In the second part Himani delineates the plight of the immigrants through Paki, a Japanese girl:

a grenade explodes
in the sunless afternoon
and words run down like frothy white spit
down her bent head
down the serene parking of her dark hair
as she stands too visible
from home to bus stop to home
raucous hyena laughter
"Paki, Go home." (7)

Though Himani Bannerji asks the immigrants to go home, yet she is also conscious of the fact that now it is not possible to go back to the homeland. Therefore, in the third part of the poem she exhorts the immigrants to accept the alien land for which they must organize lest they should suffer due to any kind of demarcation. She versifies her feelings in "Paki Go Home":

Now and then again
We must organize.
The woman wiping the slur spit
from her face, the child standing
at the edge of the playground silent, stopped.
The man twisted in despair,
disabled at the city gates.
Even the child in the womb
must find a voice
sound in unison
organize
Like a song, like a roar
like a prophecy that changes the world. (6)

Next, Himani Bannerji emphasizes on unison, "soul breathed in/ Until she, he/ the young, the old is whole" (6). She consistently asks to act with wisdom to regain the past in the alien land. Similarly in Laksmi Gill's *Retuning the Empties,* there is a quite curiosity about change. "I don't know when it got away from me/ or if I even had a say in it, say,/ a little say in its transformations..." ("I Turn" 47). The collection is a life's chronicle, especially the chronicle of an immigrant's life and consciousness. The poems reduplicate the journey from past to the present and yearning of which Gill speaks in her epilogue, "Pooja for Papa":

Somewhere may be in Hoshiarpur
in his village Posi,
the ashes that flowed from Stanley Park waters
have found a river there
rested there in its depth in fluvial tendrils.
A final rest
beyond my imaginings, in that village
I dream of on solitary nights
in this foreign city
when my heart pauses as his face forms in the dark
and his voice assures me:
Someday you will see India,
you will come home, you will know home,
you will flow back into your beginnings. (28)

M.G. Vassanji puts this predicament in *No New Land* in the following way: "We are but creatures of our origins and however stalwartly we march forward, paving new roads, shaping new works; the ghosts from our past stand not far behind and are not easily shaken" (9). Ronald Sutherland puts this fact by suggesting that the diasporic writers, "distil their experiences of Canada through a rich variety of rich cultural heritage. Perhaps it is this very process of diverse cultural distillation that will become the distinctive characteristic of Canadian literature" (76).

The third phase of the world of diasporic poets is the phase of reconciliation, first with the self and with the new land. Here it is remarkable to note that these poems give incredible evidence of their assertion, affirmation and protest in an alien land. Now the linear narrative of home and exile charts the complex journey of the poet who has moved from despair and pessimism to reconciliation and acceptance. In "Homecoming" the poet unfolds this journey in the following way:

> the journey's throbbing walk
> to this igloo of heaven
> or that sun-faced island of the elephant
> where I am always at home. (Crusz 43)

The diasporic poetry in Canada portrays a relationship to the new homeland. It represents a new power from the poets' keen observation of life and people. There is a modulating voice that narrates and describes the varied experiences of the diasporic poets, and an implicit determination to face the challenges of discrimination—sometimes with humour and compassion, but more often through a global understanding of race, gender and class in Canada. Crusz takes us to the very heart of the immigrant's story, from bewildered dislocation in the poems like "Sun-Man in Suburbia" to bewildered reconciliation in the poems like "The Rain Doesn't Know Me Any More".

The diasporic poets see a birth of a new relationship. This can be exemplified from a bilingual collection of poems, *No More Watno Dur* of Sadhu Binning, a poet of Indian diaspora in Canada. Binning's poems chart out the journey, suggested by the title *No More Watno Dur* ("no longer far from the homeland"). There are two poems "River Relations" and "No More Watno Dur" which sit at the centre of this volume both literally and figuratively. These two poems invoke the ritual immersion of his father's ashes not in the Ganga, the Yamuna, or the Satluj, but in the icy cold waters of the Squamish river. These poems have two important things—the ritual and the letter the poet writes to his family in India about the death of his father. The ritual and the letter represent his new link to Canada. As Binning sees it, the letter "written/from my country to another country" (No More Wanto Dur 26) as "one rupturing relationship gives birth to new one" (River Relations 45). The poet views the river ritual as signaling a shift in his immigrant life. As he immerses the remains of his dead father in the Canadian river, "The strangeness of the place melted/ a personal image now flows in memory/ perhaps that's what my father meant/ by relation of rivers to them" (45).

The immigrants who thought "Countryless, orphaned, scurvy ridden sailors" (Gill *Home* 19) and "had thrown away the charts/ caught in the doldrums" (*Home* 19) now see, think and feel deeply turning their estrangement and pain into understanding and insight. There is a return from a geographic space of the spirit to the reality of the new homeland, i.e. Canada. It underlines the process of adaptation to the new homeland which immigrants undergo:

> The land is home to me
> Now homeless, a true refugee
> Of the soul's last corner
> Sadhu days, and babu days
> And Mai in ohrni days
> Lost to me—like elephants
> And silks, the dhows of Naipaul's
> Yearning, not mine. (Espinet. *Hosay Night* 10)

Ever aware of the power of nostalgia to eliminate negative memories and enshrine the positive, Crusz yearns for "the green land/ forever green/ the lost country/ ever perfect" (*Elephant and Ice* 21) but soon comes to know that such a place exists only in memory and so living in Canada, he accepts that "The white marshmallow land/ is now mine, conquered,/ cussed upon loved" (*Elephant and Ice* 22). Now the feelings of nostalgia and the Canadian consciousness mix together and lead to the process of acculturation and adjustment. The expression seems to say that the immigrants and the poets fully inhabit the space, and not return empties but plentitude.

WORKS CITED

Bannerji, Himani. *Doing Time.* Toronto: Sister Vision Press, 1986.

Binning, Sadhu. *No More Watno Dur.* Toronto: TSAR, 1994.

Brand, Dionne. *Chronicles of the Hostile Sun.* 1984.

Crusz, Rienzi. *The Insurgent Rain: The Selected Poems 1974-1996.* Toronto: TSAR, 1997.

Espinet, Ramabai. *Nuclear Seasons.*

Gill, Lakshmi. *Returning the Empties: Selected Poems 1960-1990.* Toronto: TSAR, 1998.

Kalsey, Surjeet. *Footprints of Silence*, 1988.

Parameswaran, Uma. *Trishanku and Other Writings.* New Delhi: Prestige, 1998.

Said, Edward. *Culture and Imperialism.* London: Vintage, 1994.

Sutherland, Ronald. "The Mainstream of Canadian Literature." *A Meeting of Streams: South Asian Canadian Literature*, 1985.

Vassanji, M.G. *No New Land.* Toronto: McClelland and Stewart Inc., 1991.

Dialectics of Culture/ Acculturation in Bharati Mukherjee's *Jasmine* and Anita Desai's *Journey to Ithaca*

3

O.P. Budholia

The passionate search for seeking and accomplishing the roots of national culture or the essence of nativism sometimes create the sense of differences and dissension. It seems that people in spite of having racial superiority, traditional wealth, the definitive geographic advantages, linguistic and ethnic heritage and territorial bounds, die for the sake of native cause. Now, the determinants of that particular cause or essence is hard to be defined; perhaps the nuclear of the essence lies in culture. The intense desire to seek and to accomplish the native (*Desi*) values as propounded by the social-moral psyche becomes the prime motif for solving the question of culture. To fight for national culture means to liberate nation itself from the colonial effects. Thus, to save, to accomplish and to explain national culture means to define the national psyche on which the pulsating nerve of the entire nation rotates.

Indian English literature raises some questions before the writers: the question of its narratology which includes again a question of how India should be narrated in its writing especially the narrations of its culture. There are some writers such as Kamala Markandaya, Bharati Mukherjee and others who married English gentlemen and lived in U.K. and U.S.A. There are some like Shiv K. Kumar, Saros Cowasjee, Bhabani Bhattacharya, A.K. Ramanujan and others who either studied in European countries or are staying there. It is evident that these writers are the product of two cultures; they sometimes feel an inner strife between their cognition and perception. Here cognition stands for their *sanskars* which have made their personality up till they moved to any alien country. Hindu philosophy and ethics teach that right action for an individual depends on *desa,* the culture in which he is born; on *kala,* the period of historical time in which he lives; on *srama,* the efforts and on *gunas,* the innate psychobiological traits which are the heritage of an individual's previous lives. An association between social configurations and the inherited *sanskars* make one's culture strong. The Hindu or Indian culture—

> like the evidence of the senses which more often than not goes unquestioned, the metareality of a culture is also rarely summoned for conscious examination; yet it exercises an influence on individual thought and behaviour that is somewhat comparable to the working of the reality and pleasure principles. Instinctual and reality demands, it seems, have their counterpart in cultural imperatives. Denial of these imperatives can create tension and disease in the individual. (Kakar 51)

The difference between the Eastern and the Western cultures is that in the Eastern (Hinduism) guilt is related to man's ignorance for comprehending his own nature while in the Western culture it is related to the sinfulness of sexual love. However, the text of this paper deals with the theoretic norms of diasporic sensibility as the issues of isolation, alienation, dislocation, exilement in the two Indian English novels—*Jasmine* (1991) by Bharati Mukherjee and *Journey to Ithaca* (1995) by Anita Desai.

These two novels deal with the enigmatic and traumatic complexities of human behaviour. The thought and speech related to the inner analysis of the characters in these novels become symbolic and suggestive of the dialectics of culture and the process of acculturation. For the analysis of exilement, diasporic experiences, the issues of non-shared environment and the trans-cultural process therein, the textual properties of the chosen texts will be analysed. The matter of linguistic appropriateness involves the attitude and reaction of the speakers and hearers. There is nothing intrinsic about the semantic values, from asocial point of view and "in contrast to an asocial attitude, a point was made that the semantic values are dictated by the reactions of language users to the socio-linguistic environment" (Kutty 45).

Based on the metaphor of collective memories (*semantic and episodic*), *Jasmine* becomes symbolic of the duality of cultures—the East and the West. Jyoti, the protagonist, experiments life for human feeling, intuition, sensation and the dilemma of an expatriate who voluntarily leaves India and comes to America. Mukherjee, herself marries an American, Clark Blais and undergoes the experience of diaspora. Her possessed emotion becomes symbolic of human behaviour through the medium of poetic imagination, for the creation of *Jasmine,* the novel and the protagonist immediately witness the poetic qualities of the novelist so far as the range of imagination and the objectivisation of human emotions are concerned; it solves the question of *otherness* and assimilation through the logicentric dialectics of culture. The contemporary literary writing includes mainly two aspects in its contents: politics and culture. Politics symbolizes the centre of power while the culture includes the social sharing of ideas among various communities, races and religions. This then raises another issue: the dialectics of history and it finally resects into an essence which is called historicity or the formation and re-formation of the processed identity of an individual, society and nation as a whole. The woman too shares her contribution to the processed identity of a nation, so far as the narration of a nation in a literary genre is concerned:

> This relation between the nation and the novel is more acute in the case of women's writings. For a long period of time the state, the language, the patriarchal elite culture posed as if she was not there—not as human being. Thus, women were always either attractive, sensuous play things or hussies and mothers. In fact, on the socio-political scene she was a show piece to be held high, a flesh piece to be violated to bring disgrace to the clan or group or nation she belongs to. Thus, a woman is always treated as an object and not as an individual. (Mitra 185)

Simple village girl, Jyoti, renamed as Jasmine in Bharati

Mukherjee's *Jasmine*, reveals socio-psychological traumas, relating to the life of an exile or expatriate. Based on mnemonic metaphor (gross form of memories as semantic and episodic), Jasmine works out the transoceanic, transmutative, transnational and transcultural issues as alien native in America. In India her marriage with Prakash Vijh absorbs her light and changes her into a modern girl, Jasmine. She thinks of accompanying her husband to America, but as luck would have it, a Sikh terrorist, Sukkhi, murders him. With the cognitive mode of exploitation in a feudal society at Hasnapur, Jyoti as Jasmine exemplifies the will of a woman who fights in order to exist first in India and then in society of America. In Indian feudal society she points out the exploitation of women when she says, "daughters were curses" (39) at Hasnapur. The association of the emotional and physical properties of the two forms of a woman—Jyoti and Jasmine bringforth some convertive reactions. The semiotic relationship presents the seminal analysis of Jyoti of Hasnapur in times to come: "Prakash had taken Jyoti and created Jasmine and Jasmine would complete the mission of Prakash. Vijh & Wife" (97).

Hasnapur as a cognitive metaphor of collective memories has been repeated several times in the text of *Jasmine* and it becomes suggestive of ethnocentric mode of a community. The astrologer at Hasnapur symbolizes the gross properties of time (time present and time past) when he foretells about Jasmine's "widowhood and exile". The chuckling forehead of Jasmine by him and leaving a permanent scar on her forehead becomes at a later stage the mythic reality of *trinetra* (third eye) of Lord Shiva:

> "it's not a scar," I shouted, "it's my third eye." In the stories that our mother recited, the holiest sages developed an extra eye right in the middle of their foreheads. Through that eye they pierced out into invisible worlds. "Now I'm a sage." (5)

With a specific cognitive mode as semantic memories, she begins her journey towards America for materializing the dream of her husband—Vijh & Wife. On the way, she was raped first in the boat and then in a hotel. The metaphor of third eye reminds her the power of a woman (*nari shakti*). She prays before the idol of Ganapati and transforms herself as Mother Kali and kills her rapist:

> No one to call to, no one to disturb us. Just me and the man who had raped me, the man I had murdered. The room looked like a slaughter house. Blood had congealed on my hands, my chin, my breasts. What a monstrous thing, what an infinitesimal thing, is the taking of a human life; for the second time in three months. I was in a room with a slain man, my body bloodied. I was walking death. Death incarnate. (119)

With the emotion of *bhaya* (fear) the poetic elements with its *sthayin* (permanent emotion), of *bibhatsa rasa* is discernible in this textual citation. This dominant emotion of fear also decides the structural mode or *prabandha vakrata* to be developed in the text of the novel. In her translocation, she comes in touch with a missionary lady, Lillian Gordon who helps Jasmine and sends her to New York. Here she finds the job of Day's Mummy in the house of Mr. Taylor. Gradually, she begins to love her master Taylor. Finally, she moves to Iowa where she comes in touch with Mr. Bud, an agriculturist. She begins to love Bud and gets pregnant by him. Mr. Bud promises to marry her soon. At the same time, her former lover Taylor comes to Iowa. The past union as the beloved of Taylor overpowers her emotionally and she leaves the company of a father like husband, Mr. Bud, for the sake of Taylor's love. She now stops to think herself as Jane—a name given to her by Bud.

Her imaginative insight makes her adjust amicably in alien country. Through her imagination, she brings the social and cultural chart of Hasnapur and reports to the readers thus: "The men in our village weren't saints. We had our incidents. Rape, ruin, shame. The women's strategy was to stick together. Stragglers, beware" (55). Here one sees the colonial and the feudal otherness of women in their own country. Jyoti, the traditional girl of Hasnapur of Punjab, finds the crumbling of her tradition in an alien culture:

> I know, and of course, the papers nowadays are full of caste-no-bar-divorcees-welcome matrimonial ads, but

> it seems to me that once you let one tradition go all the other traditions crumble. (75)

Intent on the specific cognitive behaviour of Hasnapur, Jasmine experiences the pangs emanating from the association of two cultures: one that she inherits from the feudal society of Hasnapur of Punjab; and the other she receives from the unshared environment of America. Hasnapur as a semiotic text becomes the seminal analysis in *Jasmine.* Her husband Prakash symbolises for the change in her feudal thinking [Don't crawl back to Hasnapur and feudalism, that Jyoti is dead" (96)]. A catalyst agent for objectifying human emotions, she brings forth the modernization of the Hindu culture by comparing the statements of her uncle and her husband:

> For the uncle, love was control. Respect was obedience. For Prakash, love was letting go. Independence, self-reliance. I learned the litany by heart. But I felt suspended between worlds. (76)

There comes a strife inner due to the native sensibility or *marga* as culture and the association with a culture of non-shared community in Europe. However, the pragmatic vision of Prakash is so writ large as the code of her inner psyche that she breaks the traditional bonds of society of Hasnapur for realizing the dream of Vijh & Wife. She undergoes the metamorphosis of many names such as *Jyoti, Jasmine, Kali, Jassy, Jase, Juhane* and *Jane.* Almost in all her names, capital/J/occurs except/K/in Kali. Consonant/J/stands for *jagrukta* (awareness) of her femaleness while consonant/K/symbolizes *Kal* in the form of *Kali.* It shows that she becomes aware of the dialectics of history, culture and the cyclic movement of time. Thus, she decodes the oblique and the complicated code of history and culture. The dialectics of culture as "sign" traces minutely the process of signifier and signified. She narrates the dialectics of history and culture through the words of a terrorist, Sukkhi. Sukkhi calls "all Hindu women whores, all Hindu men rapists" (65). In his reply to Prakash, Sukkhi narrates the cultural differences between Hindus and Muslims and the relationship of Muslims with Sikhs:

> True Pakistanis are Punjabis, like us. If they were cruel to Sikhs it's because of Hindu influence on them. Many of them had Hindu mothers and Hindu concubines who taught them to kill Sikhs. Pakistanis were Hindus who saw the light of the true God and converted. So were Sikhs. Only bloodsucker *banyas* and untouchable monkeys remained Hindu. (66)

The *vacyartha* or sign of this passage, occurs in the evils of casteism which forbade the racial amiability.

Hasnapur recedes gradually from the conscious mind of Jasmine in alien culture, however, the continuum of cognition as unconscious remains operative in the psyche of Jasmine. Though Jasmine acknowledges her rootedness in America: "I was landed in getting rooted" (179) yet the cognition of Hasnapur still decides the structural plan of the novel. Hasnapur as the unconscious is linked with the process of culture and with the seminal analysis of the protagonist. The clash between her culture and nature as a woman produces the concept of cross-culturalism. The gross memories (semantic and episodic) of Hasnapur become her national identity which comes in clash with European culture. In spite of some social and psychological differences of nationalism, the association of the two creates the third one—the composite culture of the East and the West.

It is through her cognized mode of India, Jasmine works out the theory of *karma* and *kal* (Time). For the theory of *karma,* she brings forth the unconscious mode of her thinking. She says, "my grandmother may have named me Jyoti, light, but in surviving I was already Jane, a fighter and adapter" (40). As a "mystery inscrutability", the fighter Jane becomes submissive before the powerful yet unseen hands of Time. She swings without any certainty between real and human time which make her disillusioned between the reality and *maya* (illusion) of time. As a fighter and adapter, and even after so many transformation of herself into different names, she still enquires, "Who I am" (197). She quotes the words of Karim who says about her: "I am tornado.... How many more shapes are in me, how many more selves, how many more husbands" (215). Here she expresses the inner pangs of an exile and expatriate who lives in America. At the instance of an Indian woman, she submits her person to the unseen and unrealized bounds of Time:

> Then there is nothing I can do. Time will tell if I am a tornado, rubble maker, arising from nowhere and disappearing into a cloud. (241)

The next novel chosen for analysing journey image is Anita Desai's *Journey to Ithaca.* The contemporary Indian English writers are in the quest of a pattern of their narrative. Indian writers feel a kind of obsession between *Marga* and *Desi* theories even in India. Thus, they still feel the complexities of narration between tradition and modernity:

> Traditional forms were not viewed in isolation as individual entities in themselves—they functioned in the company of each other and were brought alive in a participatory interaction with the audience.... Each tradition carried elements of the other and functioned in the twilight zone of a *sandhyabhasa* arousing multiple association simultaneously. (Sheikh 265)

If the traditional form stands for *desivad,* its association with *Marga* (classical) seems an inevitable step. In isolation it can't function properly. Thus, the theory of *Marga* and *Desi* are complimentary and becomes representative of expressing the nativism in literature.

The theories of *Desi* and *Marga* can be traced in the text of *Journey to Ithaca.* Discipleship of a Muslim girl, Laila is challenged in the *ashram* of her Guru; and this kind of opposition works out the theory *of marga.* The root *of marga* is in its root words *marg* and *mrg* which denote their English synonyms as "track" and "forest animal" respectively. The term "desi" brings into being the local talents, coming out of the traditional pattern of a particular ethnic group or community:

> Thus *desi* is whatever is available in a given form in the world and it came to be applied to language, literature, metres, music, dance etc. as available in the community and inherited by tradition. In contrast *marga* came to be applied to what is structured, refined and

> ornamented.... But the dichotomy is found in every aspect of the human faculty and hence can be spoken of even with reference to ritual, religion, philosophy, beliefs and customs. (Murti 61)

In common parlance, the terms *marga* and *desi* become symbolic for the theory of nativism.

Out of the three main characters in the text of *Journey to Ithaca,* the two Matteo and Laila come to India willingly for experiencing the higher vision of human life. Matteo's wife Sophie comes under social compulsions and she hardly associates with Indian sensibility in various *ashrams.* Thus, both Sophie and Matteo had a design, a pattern to their wanderings. After her first delivery she develops dissension and differences with Matteo and comes back to Italy. But after some time she comes to India again and enquires of the past life of Laila. As a woman with woman's jealousy, she regards mother "a monster spider who had spun this web to catch these silly flies" (7). Disagreeing with Matteo, Sophie asserts that "she may be your mother but I don't need this one" (127). After her second delivery, she comes to Italy again and tries to seek her love in Matteo's friend Paolo. But she fails to have it: "Her life with Matteo had spoilt her life with a man like this Paolo; it was no longer possible" (229). Coming back to India, she collects all the facts about the past life of Laila. But when she desires to follow the path of her husband, she does not find him in the *ashram.* With the metamorphosis of her personality, she finally confesses to Diya about her *bhava parivartan* (spiritual change).

As an exile, Laila brings into being at the instance of Sri Aurobindo's *Savitri,* some distinction between pragmatism of the West and the spiritual wisdom of the East. Daughter of Alma and Hameed, Laila rebels against the restrictions of Muslim religion. She was sent first to Cairo and then to Paris for her higher studies. As a leader at Al-Azhar University, she awakens her fellow students—"better to go to prison than live as slaves" (171). Of course, in learning and performing the classical dance of India in *Krishna Lila,* she realizes the spiritual power and goes beyond the range of human senses. With the complete belongingness, she becomes an example for the humanistic vision of *desivad* in the *ashram* as Mother. She finally leaves even the troupe of *Krishna Lila*. As a *sadhaka* and as a native of Alexandria, she comes to the *ashram* of Swami Premanand Ji. Here, she faces the wrath of orthodox Hindu *sadhaka* for her entry in the *ashram*; but her teacher on humanistic ground supports Laila's "search after truth" (207). On the protest of orthodox *sadhakas*, Swamiji shifts his *ashram* and comes to another place in the Himalayan region and here he assigns the status of Motherhood to Laila. On the example of Kabir, a Muslim saint, Swamiji supports Laila's quest for higher vision of life.

In *Marga-Desi* theory, the *marga* stands for all that is "conventional (samyika) assigned (*samketika*), and formal (*parinisthita*), while *desi* is natural (*svabhavika*), unassigned (*asamketika*). "Conflict resolves in agreement and diversity begets unity" (8). Laila as Mother and preacher to her disciples in the *ashram* distinguishes between two approaches: *Marga* and *Desi*:

> This is no church, my friends, this is no temple or mosque or vihara. We have no religion. Religion? Like the black crows up in the tree, caw-caw-caw scolding, scolding. But do they crow at us now. No, they are silent. We have silenced them! Religion makes one ashamed, makes one guilty, makes one fearful. The Master has told you not to feel guilty, not to feel ashamed, not to be afraid. Open your hearts to love and light and the joy of loving.... (98)

Along with the theory of *Desi* and *Marga, Journey to Ithaca* also works out the theory of universal consciousness. Even the scientists make the assertion that "the body did not create the mind; the mind evolved much before the physical body and composed the neuronic and biochemical brain mechanisms to use as its tool" (Kundu 14). The Indian philosophic system too works out the seven great modifications for the existence of matter in a solar system. The first three of these seven modifications are: the physical, emotional (astral) and mental. They are called *Triloki* or *Tribhuvanam* (three worlds).

Any *sadhaka* has to undergo the pangs of these three world in his/her inner journey. They are helpful only in normal evolution of humanity. Overcoming the bounds of *Tribhuvanam,* the *sadhaka* enters the fourth, *buddhic* (intelligence) and then the *atmic.* These five through their mutual combinations are helpful to the evolution of consciousness. The evolutionary process goes on until the being merges finally into the existence of divine. The remaining two *anupada* and *adi* beyond the level of five represent the sphere of divine activity, encircling and enveloping all, out of which come out the divine energies. As the "sign" of divine consciousness, the highest becomes the source for *creation, preservation* and *dissolution* (10).

Laila's journey begins from the elemental realities, but reaches to the spiritual height of human evolution. The causative being as catalyst experiences the manifestation of the Supreme Self. In her upward height to Godhead, Laila, the mother, experiences as the sensations of her lower impulses. Even Laila confesses the presence of lower impulses as the lower particles of her personality. She fights the negative forces inside and comes out triumphant as a *sadhaka.* She acknowledges the particles of her lower personality:

> I walk up and down the long Veranda looking out at the stars, and they call to me. They seem to say, Higher, climb higher. I am too weak to go climbing. The night air is cold. My shawl is thin and provides little warmth. This gives me a feeling of frailty. I need strength and courage, and then I will set out, and I will climb, and I will go up the mountain into the heights. For this, I came to India. (297)

The scientists and psychologists have proved the interconnectedness of each part of the universe which throws light on the phenomenon of consciousness. The inner longingness of Laila finally is interconnected, with the spiritual energy of her Master and thus she attains the status of sainthood as mother. She achieves the highest motifs in the company of her Guru, Premanandji:

> Sometimes my master must exist. As my life I have known of his existence and seen the *signs*...yet I have been misled because of my weakness and ignorance that made mistake what is only human for what is supreme and almighty. (256)

The concept of "sign" in this citation becomes the structural approach for the logocentric reflections of being. Her arrival in India as signifier and to follow the path of her teacher as signified deconstruct the construction of logocentric sign. She attains the highest knowledge of logos and realizes the logic of manifestations as *Adi* inside her psyche. Out of the realizations of the divine manifestations, she like *Mira* thinks of God:

> He spoke you will come and live with me within my *ashram* and by the light of the washed and silver moon, we crossed the courtyard and entered his abode. Here I dwell now where I was always meant to dwell and where I resolve to live, never leaving his side. His true devotee and lover. (302)

Thus, in both the journeys—the Journey of Jasmine and the Journey of Laila—two distinct paradigms are analysed. Journey of Jasmine comes to *bhava parivartan* (spiritual change) after material dialectics. Since the journey of Jasmine is meant for socio-psycho-historical dialectics of human thoughts, it reveals an analysis of dissociation and association of human sensibilities. She leaves a message of human exploitation, postcolonial reactions and poststructural viewpoints. The linguistic ephithets used in the text such as "tornado", "rubble maker" created the situational and contextual referents which make Jasmine a helpless being in society. The journey of Laila is out of any compulsion. She achieves what she intends to achieve and she decodes the code of the highest reality of being and becoming. Thus, both the novels work out some possibilities for objectifying the physical and spiritual norms beyond the bounds of nativism, time and space.

WORKS CITED

Desai, Anita. *Journey to Ithaca*. London: William Heinemann Ltd., 1995.
Kakar, Sudhir. *The Indian Psyche*. Delhi: Oxford University Press, 1998.

Kundu, M.N. "Beyond Body: Journey to the Centre of the Minds." *The Times of India.* New Delhi, 10 Feb., 2006.

Kutty, A.P. Andrew. "Semantics on Structural Linguistics." *Aspects of Paninian Semantics.* Ed. C. Rajendran. New Delhi: Sahitya Academi, 2002.

Mitra, Joy. "The Other Voice: Women's Writing in India." *Narrating India: The Novel in Search of the Nation.* Ed. E.V. Ramakrishnan. New Delhi: Sahitya Academi, 2005.

Mukherjee, Bharati. *Jasmine.* New York: Virago Press, 1991.

Murti, M. Srimannarayana. "Cultural Discourse–Desi and Marga." *Nativism in Criticism.* Ed. Makarand Paranjape. New Delhi: Sahitya Academi, 1997.

Bharati Mukherjee's *Jasmine*: Breaking the Silence and Weaving the Web

4

Beena Agarwal

The predicament of the fate of the females in cross-cultural spaces has been a major component of the literature produced by writers, surviving in the conflicting pulls of "home" and "homelessness", passing through the voyage of migration to assimilation. The consistent confrontation in the process of assimilation, stumbling against alien cultural forces with the persisting shadows of native cultural heritage, fractures the individual's self, generating only a greater isolation and loneliness. Bharati Mukherjee with her consciousness of the dilemma of cultural crisis shares the anguish and suffering of "Womanhood" in the order of patriarchy. Most of the protagonists of Bharati Mukherjee, besides preserving their essential "feminity", endeavour to protect their womanhood and individuality in the cultural surroundings, chosen out of personal choices or thrusted out of professional compulsions. Hence the complexity of female identities in the writers of Indian diaspora reflects distinctive dimensions yielding only a greater isolation, insecurity, sexual exploitation, violence and the triumph of male chauvinism. In the recent 'women's studies', it has been pointed out that different cultures have different structures of values, recommending the distinctive code of morality for women. However, in spite of certain cultural distinctions of East and West, feminism still holds that there is a universal sisterhood where women, regardless of cultural disparities, have something in common. The real feminism consists in the experience of being a 'woman'. Bharati Mukherjee's fictional world is an account of women experiences in different cultural spaces, seeking a common conclusion that the realisation of being a woman and the unconditional surrender of a woman to the tributes of feminity are the integral part of feminine psyche. She exposes women's silence, resistance, oppression against the order of patriarchy, horror of rape, the phobea of pregnancy, craving for male companionship, as the experiences common both to native heritage and the cultural surroundings of the country of their migration.

In the novel *Jasmine,* the protagonist Jasmine appears as an innocent village girl, unaware of the traditional ways of the world but is sufficiently conscious of her own desires and choices. Her life begins in a small village of Hasnapur, Punjab, and ends in Iowa and in this odyssey, she passes through various geographical locations and the flux of cultural identities and in this transition, she justifies herself in each and every role and sustains her basic identity of being an Indian woman. In defence of Jasmine's character, Bharati Mukherjee presents a confessional note:

> The kinds of women I write about...are those who are adaptable we've, all be raised to please, been trained to be adaptable as wives and that adaptability is working to women's advantage when we came over as immigrant. (Conned et al., 19)

Different locations assign her different roles—wife, daughter, care-taker, beloved and competent professional but at every stage she is conscious to achieve an identity of her own, along with her consciousness of her being an Indian woman. The synthesis of cultural awareness, feminist sensibility and the assertion of individuality add a new dimension to the feminist consciousness scattered in the novels of Bharati Mukherjee. She is neither a "rebel" as it has been criticised by Bharati Mukherjee herself, nor an oppressed subject but a woman with her independent vision, sharing the best both of native tradition and the occult of hi-tech of the West. It is said:

> Jasmine's liner monologues and silent reflections capture her deliberations on cultural differences and on immigrant women's emotional adherence to her traditional beliefs while intellectually exploring the

> new avenues opened to her by the modern value system. (Parekh 113)

Jasmine was born and brought up in a traditional family of Punjab, where women were conditioned to maintain the perpetual silence against the order of patriarchy where the only purpose of girl's life was to find out "cut-rate" husbands. The inferiority groups, her psyche, born out of two complexes—her existence as a woman and her subaltern status for being a "village girl". She makes a candid confession, "that big-city men prefer us village girls because we are brought up to be caring and have no minds of our own. Village girls are like cattle, whichever way you lead them, that is the way they will go" (39). The rooted images of subjugated status are the manifestation of the disgust for the gender bias existing at the core of Indian cultural colonialism. Her ability to write the "Best English Composition" was of no worth in Indian family. Her grandmother finally located a possible groom, a widower with three children to take her off. Jasmine in spite of her traditional upbringing nourishes her own dreams of life. She expresses her first independent thinking, "I want to be a doctor and set up my own clinic in a big town" (45) but her high ambitions were treated only as her madness. "The girl is mad. Her mother is mad. The whole country is mad. *Kali-yuga* has already come" (45). After the death of her father, she was stupefied, looking at the humiliation of her mother who tried to throw herself on the funeral pyre, shaved her head and wrapped her body in coarse cloth.

Jasmine enters new dimensions of relationships and cultural diversities with a specific set of mind inherited from her conventional family. She comes in contact with Prakash, a confident professional who had a dynamic vision of life. The confidence and dynamism, stirred by Prakash, brings a better acceptance of life but it was of no avail to her to exempt her from the guilt of being a girl for "no dowry and no guests". In the company of Prakash, all the time she was in grip of the fear of 'exile' and 'widowhood'. The cultural constraints that constitute her psyche let her not to dissolve her identity in the unconventional progressive ways of Prakash. He wanted her to call him by his first name but Jasmine's cultural code does not promote her to do so. The endeavours of Prakash to modify her life according to his own fantacies, neglecting her cultural roots, was another mode of conquest of male domination, affording no scope to express herself. His ultimate decision to change her name from 'Jyoti' to 'Jasmine', was the first challenge to her self-respect and self-identity. Prakash appreciates her by saying, "You are small and sweet and heady" but remains ignorant of the terrible flow of emotions going on within her innerself. The anguish is well expressed in the confession: "he wanted to break down the Jyoti, I'd been in Hasnapur and make me a kind of city woman. To break off the past, he gave me a new name: Jasmine" (70). In Jasmine's case, the truth is to be admitted that even before entering the trans-cultural spaces and encountering the trauma of immigration, her integrated psyche was shattered, "Jyoti, Jasmine: I shuttled between identities" (70). Prakash not only controls her external life but also the private matters related with the experiences of being a female. She has a longing to conceive a child but the decision regarding the pregnancy was not her choice but the prerogative of Prakash. The 'rebel' starts taking place within her innerself. Her resentment is evident in her confession, "you think hi-tech solves every problem. What does hi-tech say about a woman's need to be a mother?" (70) Jasmine clamors for the love and company of Prakash but buried her desires in perpetual silence. "I missed him, but I didn't feel abandoned" (72). In both the extremes of the ideologies of Prakash, she finds herself lost in the web of illusions. She recalls the words of her mother who used to say that a husband has layers like an onion. Prakash is excited on the idea of a 'real-life', the fantasy of migration to America, a land of hi-tech culture. His dreams do not correspond with the choices of Jasmine. He contemptuously snubs Jasmine, "Caring only about pregnancies". All the time Prakash imposes his own authority, "Don't crawl back to Hasnapur and Feudalism. That Jyoti is dead" (87). Such an helplessness of Jasmine is the manifestation of the persistent conflict within the mind of a woman—the conflict of her own individuality and the calls of feminity. In a sudden attack of Khalsa Lion, Prakash is killed and Jasmine is left lonely, desolate and an unfortunate widow.

In her associations with Prakash, Jasmine represents genuine human emotions. In her conflict, there is a combination of traditional mother who has an inherent urge to sustain her womanhood but is a 'rebel' against the conventions that restrain the realization of the individuality of a woman.

The second phase of Jasmine's life begins after her migration to America. For her the shelter in America was a mode to escape the shadows of the past, the process to ensure a renewed identity, the canvas that affords a greater scope for emancipation and the fulfillment of the dreams of her deceased husband. It was unfortunate that her first exposure to American life in an alien culture marked by opulence and exhibition only proves a web of illusions and humiliations. After her first landing at America, she was received by the captain of the ship known as Half Face, representative of the dirt of underworld. He tried to take benefit of her weaker position for being a woman as well as being an 'Ignorant Indian'. On his attempt of sexual humiliation, she pathetically implores, "my husband was killed, please don't do anything to me" (102). The rebellion born out of horrors of rape, generates violence within her. She sliced her tongue and with blood dripping tongue, she stabbed Half Face. Jasmine's recourse to violence was neither a lunacy nor a crime but it was the external manifestation of irresistible contempt for the conditions over which she had no control. Had it not been so, she might have committed suicide or might have been a lunatic. Rape is the worst horror for a woman, a desperate realisation of her position as 'ABALA', more than being social injustice, it is a state of mind where calm resistance is likely to be transmuted in any extreme form. In Jasmine's case, the murder of Half Face was a mode of revenge no doubt, but it was also a method of justice though it may be wild. To quote:

> Rape after all is an omnipresent terror to all women of any class, race or caste. *Baltry* is the nightmare of the emotional and physical pain no matter who is the victim. (Morgan 4)

Samir Dayal in his article "Creating, Preserving, Destroying: Violence in Bharati Mukherjee's *Jasmine*", makes a very appropriate observation:

> This catastrophic violence that lies just beneath the skin of the quotidian is meticulously but offhandedly catalogued by Jasmine as though to banalize it, as though the victims, the perpetrators and the observers of the violence were benumbing or anaesthetizing themselves against an excess of reality. (73)

Jasmine's recourse to violence ascertains that Bharati Mukherjee nowhere takes women's 'silence' as a mode of weakness. In the article "Sexual Class in India", Mody and Mahtre have categorically pointed out that women are capable and incapable of 'speaking' depending upon the circumstances. In the feminist discourse, the women speaking in the mode of social mechanism which represses women is not the 'feminist voice', it depends on consciousness. This consciousness comes from outside when women "are encouraged to voice their resentment to identify their oppressors and to struggle to improve their conditions". Ever since this incident, Jasmine instead of taking recourse to self-accusation and self-pity, proceeds in the direction of reincarnation, a new woman who has her own dreams and ambitions, infinite potentiality to resist the irrational control of patriarchy and a quest for self-identity. Sushila Singh in her speculative discourse appreciates this positive thrust of life in the female protagonists of Bharati Mukherjee:

> Bharati Mukherjee's women characters offer a frontal challenge to patriarchal thought, social organisation and control mechanism expose her underlying passive violence. (65)

In Bharati Mukherjee's fictional world, the flux of identities and cultural diversities make no discrimination in the experiences specific to feminine sensibility. Jasmine's second encounter with Lillian Gordon in California adds new dimensions to her consciousness. After the horrible memories of rape and murder, the maternal care of Lillian Gordon gives a new strength and purpose in the life of Jasmine. She starts calling her "jazzy" and such a loving and informal address encourages her to resume a new spring in her life. She comments, "she represented to me the best in the American experience and the American character" (121). In Jasmine's odyssey, the third encounter was with

Davendra Vadhera, the Professorji with whom she wanted to realise the dream of the real life. In her interaction with Professor Vadhera, Jasmine sustains the modesty that is expected from an "Indian widow". The irony is apparent that in spite of her feminine sensibility, she wants to obliterate her past reflecting the horrible shadows of Indian widow and seeks the opportunity for the assimilation in the dynamic and progressive society of America where sexual moral codes are not so tight fisted. On the one hand she has a dream, "I wanted to distance myself from everything Indian everything Jyoti like" (128) but at the same time the inferiority of being a woman haunts her, "to them, I was a widow who should show a proper modesty of appearance and attitude" (128). Hilda David mentions this fact in the following words:

> Sexuality of an Indian woman is well guarded by her old tradition and culture in spite of modernity in form of fashions. (79)

In spite of Professorji's love and support, Jasmine finds herself nervous for her helplessness to understand soap operas and game shows. It thrusts Jasmine to the traditional domestic responsibilities like cooking, shopping, cleaning and passing her time in the company of old folks. Such a pattern of living, instead of bringing any consolation in her life, brings a greater frustration and resentment. Her sobbing in the company of Professorji is suggestive of the emotional pressure on her mind. She has a desire to carve out her own spaces, the quest to find an identity for herself. Instead retreating in the past, she has an enlightenment, "I didn't feel safe going outdoors. If I had a Green Card, a job, a goal, *happiness* would appear out of the blue" (132) and in the same breath she said, "I told him I wanted a Green Card, more than anything else in the world that Green Card was freedom." (132) Most of the female protagonists of Bharati Mukherjee adopt the process of assimilation as the only possible remedy to break the shackles of conventionalism and to obliterate the past. For them freedom and immigration become synonymous. The enlightenment in Jasmine's life is at two levels—the awareness of her weaker position to face the trauma of social life, the awareness of the expanded horizon of human life. She fails to appreciate secretiveness and parsimoniousness of Professorji even with his wife Nirmala. Regarding his attitude she remarks, "he was following an ancient prescription for marital accord: silence, order, authority. So was she: submission, beauty, innocence" (134). In all these three relationships discussed so far, she comes to the realisation that a woman can hardly dream of an emancipated and independent identity.

In another shift of location, Jasmine comes in the family of Tylor and Wylie and it opens a new phase in the life of Jasmine. It provides an opportunity to explore instinctive urge of motherhood, hidden in the self of Jasmine. She was appointed as a caregiver for their daughter Duff. Jasmine craves for her individuality but does not hesitate to bear the burden of womanhood. In Indian society, motherhood is not confined to the bonds of biological kinship, but it is a comprehensive realisation, a specific state of mind peculiar to feminine sensibility. Jasmine seeks new cultural spaces but sustains her Indianness in terms of values and morality. As soon as Wylie reveals her that Duff is an adopted child, she finds herself confused, "I could not imagine a non-genetic child" (151). Along with Duff, she also attracts the attention of Tylor for her affectionate nature. It is specific in Jasmine's case that in spite of her native upbringing, she is free from the burden of guilt and shame. She is disgusted at the naked display of nudity in American society but has no guilt on what she had done with Half-Face. In Indian society gender relations are very tight fisted, almost a 'close door' culture but Jasmine has a clear headed approach in her relationship of love and sex. She admits, "the love I felt for Tylor that first day had nothing to do with sex. I fell in love with his world, its ease, its careless confidence and graceful self-absorption" (151). In case of Jasmine marriage, love and sex, if not independent are inter-dependent variables. When Wylie addresses her as a "caregiver", she gets the first realisation of her own "self identity", an identity different from being Prakash's wife or Vadhera's dependent, "I was a professional, like a school-teacher or a nurse. I wasn't a maid-servant" (155). Jasmine with her confidence, infinite zest for life, her dreams of future, emerges as a *New Woman*. She does not prefer to crush her individuality in the burden of tradition and persues the mission of assimilation, "But Jyoti was now a *sati*-goddess; she had burned herself in a trash-can funeral pyre behind a boarded up motel in Florida. Jasmine lived for the future, for Vijh & Wife. Jase went to movies and lived for today" (156). With the help of Tylor, she got a job for herself at Columbia in Mathematics Department. With Columbia employment, she was eligible for free tuition in Columbia extension course. Further she got an employment in Indian Language Department as Punjabi instructor. It was the realisation of her potentiality as a competent professional. In Iowa, she comes in contact of Bud and his mother Ripple Mayer. Jasmine endeavoured to absorb in the American life but she could never detach herself from her cultural roots. Subsequently, Tylor comes close to Jasmine and wants to have sexual relations with her. Jasmine has no guilt in this relationship because she comes to the realisation that each male possesses an inherent desire to rule the body of women—may it be out of love, contempt or revenge. The comment of Jasmine reflects her pain, anguish and contempt for the identical male obsession, "I have had a husband for each of the women, I have been. Prakash for Jasmine, Tylor for Jase, Bud for Jane, Half-Face for Kali" (175).

Jasmine's voyage in the different cultural spaces with her shifting identities, connecting within it the quest to realise her perfect individuality irrespective of geographical locations in order of patriarchy, is the central motif in the life of Jasmine. The novel, *Jasmine*, is an argument to set that affirmative approach to life which offers better possibility of assimilation. Jasmine escapes from Punjab to get rid of her subjugated position and to challenge the prophetic curse, anticipated to her but in fact it was her conscious effort to reject everything that hampers the growth of her creative-self. Mukherjee felt that she should have given the heroine of New York, a society, opportunity to survive. Her gradual merger into different cultures provides a testimony to the fact that she got freedom. Relph Crane points out:

> While the female protagonists of her first two novels are identified in their title by their relationship to their fathers or their husbands—a clear indication of "the restrictions imposed" on them culturally because of their gender—the heroine of this third novel has gradually refused to accept "invisibility" and ultimately rejects imperial shackles.

It is true that in Vadhera's household, Jasmine does not relish the depressing attitude of Professor Vadhera because she is destined to rediscover and reinvestigate her own innerself. Her merger in her new cultural identities is the celebration of her own freedom. Fakrur Alam is more tolerant in his tribute of Jasmine:

> By making her heroine triumph over widowhood and by depicting her opting for a fate different from what seemed to be in store for her sisters, Mukherjee is making a kind of feminist statement in the novel; women can make a difference in their lives even if they cannot cheat fate completely. (155)

For Jasmine her assimilation comes as a beautiful fabric of complete feminity and complete individuality. Jasmine nowhere makes a compromise with her identity as a woman and identity as an Indian. She shares the common emotional longing as a beloved, mother and daughter. She was conscious for her career and self-dignity. To Jasmine the flux of cultural spaces affords a wider canvas to weave fine fabric of life to escape the web of illusion of feminity, may be inside the traditional society of India and Iowa. In *Jasmine* feminity and individuality are not at crossroads. She seeks an ambivalence. To quote:

> Mukherjee has gone out her way to distance herself from American feminists in her portrayal of Jasmine by making her not only into someone who ultimately wants to do the right things for herself, no matter what that will do to others, but also into someone who tries very hard to please others and be as feminine as possible. (Alam 115)

WORKS CITED

Alam, Fakrur. "The Exuberance of Immigration." *Bharati Mukherjee*. Ed. Twayne. United Author's Series No. 635: 1996.

Conned, Michael et. al. "An Interview with Bharati Mukherjee." *Iowa Review*, No. 3 (Spring 1990).

Crane, Relph J. "Of Shattered Pots and Sinkholes: Female Identity in Bharati Mukherjee *Jasmine*." Sixth SPACLALS Triennial Conference, Freemantle, Western Australia. 9-11 December 1992.

David, Hilda. *Love and Sex in the Novels of Ruth Jhabvala*. New Delhi: Prestige Publication, 1999.

Dayal, Samir. "Creating, Preserving, Destroying: Violence in Bharati Mukherjee's *Wife* and *Jasmine*." *Bharati Mukherjee: Critical Perspective*. Ed. Emmanuel S. Nelson. New York: Garland Publishing, 1993.

Mody, S. and S. Mahtre. *Sexual Class in India*. BCHS Vol. 7, No. 1, 1975.

Morgan, Robin. *Sisterhood in Global*. Harmonsworth, 1984.

Parekh, Pushpa N. "Telling Her Tale: Narrative Voice and Gender Roles in Bharati Mukherjee's *Jasmine*." *Bharati Mukherjee: Critical Perspective*. Ed. Emmanuel S. Nelson.

Singh, Sushila. Recent Trends in Feminist Thought. *Indian Women Novelist.*, Set I, Vol. I, Ed. R.K. Dhawan. New Delhi: Perstige Publication, 1991.

Negotiating Multiculturalism in Bharati Mukherjee's *Desirable Daughters*

5

Abha Shukla Kaushik

Bharati Mukherjee is an established voice of the Indian diaspora in North America. In a critical and creative career that spans over thirty years, she has been engaged in redefining the idea of diaspora as a process of gain, contrary to the conventional perspectives that construe immigration and displacement as a condition of loss and dispossession as a result of dissolution of original culture and an erasure of history. In her fictional works she takes up the issue of the impact of expatriation and immigration on the complexities of life as pitched against divergent ethnic, religious and cultural backgrounds. Her fictions are constructed around the realities of transplantation and the resultant psychological metamorphosis of characters, brought about by crossing into another country, which is North America in her works. Her characters belong to divergent ethnic backgrounds and national origins: economic and political refugees from Afghanistan, Uganda, Iraq and Bangladesh; illegal stowaways from Ludhiana; professionals from Bombay and Calcutta; mail order brides from Nepal; and domestic helps from Trinidad. One fact, that binds them together despite their disparate cultural histories and social differences, is their shared experience of diaspora as they explore new ways of belonging and 'becoming' in America. They are America's new 'middlemen' as epitomized in the title of Mukherjee's 1988 collection of short stories the "not quite(s)".

Like her characters in diaspora, "with sentimental attachments to a distant homeland but no real desire for permanent return" (Intro. to *Darkness* xv), Mukherjee locates the trajectory of her identity and cultural politics in the course of crossing and recrossing multiple borders of language, history, race, time and culture. Disrupting the constraints and absolutisms of nationalist boundaries, her writings of diaspora embody her sense of what, as in her case, it means to be a writer who was born and raised in India, has been a citizen of Canada and the United States, and who has been shaped and transformed by the cultures of India and North America. Mukherjee herself elucidates her aesthetic stand on the identity reformulations made possible by diaspora and its contexts in terms that involve a journey from "unhousement" to "rehousement", a process that entails "breaking away from the culture into which one was born, and in which one's place in society was assured" and "re-rooting oneself in a new culture" (Hancock 39). "In this age of diasporas", she argues, "one's biological identity may not be one's only identity. Erosions and accretions come with the act of emigration" (*American Dreamer* 4).

Mukherjee's differing experiences of diaspora in Canada and the US have influenced her and her literary productions. They lead to imaginative, textual and cultural negotiations with dominant narratives. Her stance on the discourse of national identity formation in both nations, shows that there are no simplistic ways of dealing with or responding to multiculturalism, and national identity is based on her interpretation of her experiences.

Her latest novel *Desirable Daughters* is a brilliantly woven, thoughtful and intelligent story of three Calcutta-born Brahmin upper-class sisters, renowned for their beauty, brains, wealth, and privileged position in society. Mukherjee follows their lives as they leave their conservative, sheltered childhood home, where they are inundated with culture, tradition, and values and inculcated with education by the Catholic nuns in their convent structured school and college. Two sisters emigrate to America and the other relocates to Bombay, India.

The three sisters, Padma, Parvati, and Tara, are born exactly three years apart from each other and share the same birthday. Their mother names them after goddesses, hoping they will survive and prosper, which they all do. "Sisters three are we...as alike as three blossoms on a tree. (But we are not)" (21), says Tara, the protagonist, quoting a poem.

Padma, the eldest, lives in New Jersey but is completely Indian in her attire, cuisine, and her profession as the television anchor of an Indian television program, set in Jackson Heights, Queens, run by her Indian lover, while she stays married to a man once successful, but now merely living off her fame. "In the nearly twenty-five years that she has been in the United States, she has become more Indian than when she left Calcutta. She is a "multicultural performance artist" for local schools and community centers" (94).

Parvati is totally Indian to the point of allowing her husband's relatives to be houseguests for weeks at their luxurious apartment in Mumbai with its breathtaking view of the city. Her easy life with servants, drivers, and other amenities at her disposal is funnily described by Tara, as she relates her sister's "very stressed out life".

Tara, the youngest, is the most 'un-Indian' of the three. She lives in San Francisco and is divorced from an Indian Silicon Valley dotcom millionaire Bishwapriya Chatterjee, who is an ideal to all Indian immigrants, a sort of 'ethnic' Bill Gates, for his contribution to creating a network of communication via the Internet. His friend Chester Yee and he invent a computer-routing system that makes them rich.

Tara is almost a Valley woman—a volunteer at a pre-school, a single parent of a teenage son who reveals he is gay. She also has a live-in lover Andy, a balding, red-bearded former biker, former bad-boy, Hungarian Buddhist contractor/yoga instructor. If that isn't scandalous enough for an Indian woman, Tara is also caught up in the mystery of a stranger who claims to be the bastard son of a secret alliance between her eldest sister Padma and a Bengali Christian, Ron Dey.

Discovering his connection to her family, the stranger becomes both Tara's catharsis and nemesis. By complaining to the police (here she draws a hilarious sketch of an 'ethnic' policeman—a Sikh—Jasbir 'Jack' Sidhu), she calls the so-called nephew's bluff. He retaliates by bombing her house, where her ex-husband and son are at the time.

Tara looks back at her family's past and their future and comes to terms with her history and legacy, from which she is almost separated. And yet it is a part of her psyche. As she grows and matures as a character, we are drawn to her humor, her honesty, and her blunt assessment of the two worlds between which she travels, back and forth, between being American and Indian, and also travels both on psychological and physical plane.

Multiculturalism is a theme that echoes throughout the book. Of her life in San Francisco, Tara says, "...all the neighbourhood services, except the laundries and the Japanese restaurant, are owned and staffed by crack-of-dawn rising, late-night closing Palestinians, whose shifting roster of uncles and cousins seems uniformly gifted in providing our needs and anticipating our desires" (25).

Continuing this theme, Mukherjee draws a portrait of an ethnic area Jackson Heights, to where all Indian immigrants must make their pilgrimage: "We're a billion people, but divided into so many thousands or millions of classifications that we have trouble behaving as a monolith. Yet each Indian is so densely packed with family that he or she seems to contain hundreds of competing personalities. Jackson Heights is not a Chinatown or even a Japantown on the San Francisco model.... Indian people shop collectively, but they don't live together in tight little communities.... They travel in from distant suburbs,... or from neighbouring states, everyday" (199).

By bringing together characters from various ethnic backgrounds and making them inhabit the same space, Mukherjee constructs the symbolic site of a new unified whole. It may not be a space of easy harmony but of conflict and potential tension. There are prejudices, misunderstandings and confusions among the characters due to heterogeneity in cultures, accents, histories, memories and experiences.

The novel, however, begins with the most American of all searches: the desire to trace one's ancestry. Tara is fascinated by an ancestor, her almost namesake, Tara Lata, a five-year-old girl who was a victim of the archaic custom of child marriage—a tradition that even her father, a university graduate and lawyer, willingly follows. It is 1879 and Tara Lata's wedding party is travelling in a dark jungle to rendezvous with the bridegroom's family, who instead of greeting them hurls curses at the 'bride', calling her 'unlucky' because the boy bridegroom has been bitten fatally by a snake. To save her from a life of degradation, widowhood, and shame, Tara Lata's father 'marries' her to the God of the forest, and she becomes the legendary Tree Bride. The young girl retreats to her father's house and makes it a refuge for the poor, the sick, and finally the fighters for Indian independence; she is dragged from her home in 1944 by colonial authorities, who announce her death six days later.

With this novel, Bharati Mukherjee, already a critically acclaimed author and winner of the National Book Critics Award, has established herself as a formidable writer whose works combine her pride in her Indian heritage and her gratitude at the opportunities in America. In the context of *Desirable Daughters* Jope Nyman comments that Bharati Mukherjee's fictions "rewrite the traditional immigrant story, imagining new spaces and firms of identity as a result of travel and dislocation" (53).

In keeping with her literary and ideological reinscriptions of diaspora, Mukherjee has elected to describe herself as an "American" writer and has announced through various forums that it is the cultural narrative of America that has provided the enabling site for her own identity transformations as well as those she celebrates in her fictions. Her revisionary cultural politics has aroused considerable critical interest, itself a measure of the author's rising stature.

One of the chief criticisms made against Mukherjee, especially by US-based India-born critics, is that her optimistic narration of the American saga of immigrant incarnations elides a consideration of the material realities impinging on Third World immigration, namely the role of race, class and gender in the workings of identity politics in America.

A nuanced reading of her texts and an unpacking of her terminology will reveal that Mukherjee has not been wholly uncritical of dominant ideologies in her literary and cultural imagining of the American nation.

Tara travels to the New World, but, even as she absorbs the energy and vitality of this world, her traditional worldview remains intact. Mukherjee's narrative is woven within a set parameter where Indian mysticism and fatalism stand challenged by American optimism and materialism. Mukherjee recounts the Americanization of an Indian first generation female protagonist and reveals how the path to Americanization for a non-Anglo is a difficult one. On the one hand, she faces restrictions, though indirect, imposed by the ethnic group, as a result of which her divorce remains an open secret—something that cannot and should not be discussed publicly, her sister apparently has some secrets for the same 'social' reasons; on the other hand is the disillusionment brought about by the social decay. In the novel, Mukherjee dramatizes the immediate cultural negotiations that are demanded from immigrants who come to America for economic reasons. Tara's traditional background compels her to admit that she isn't, perhaps never will be, "a modern woman" (27). Although apparently she seems to have rejected her old cultural values, she is anguished and uncertain as she keeps visiting her past which is like a refrain in the narrative not only to compare things but often also to offer judgments. Her home in San Francisco reminds her "not unhappily, of mountain resorts in India" (24), although it is also a symbol of autonomy and selfhood for her. Torn between the dual pulls of her identity she is intensely aware of her difference. She says "I am not the only blue-jeaned woman with a Pashmina shawl around my shoulders and broken-down running shoes on my feet. I am not the only Indian on the block. All the same, I stand out, I'm convinced. I don't belong here, despite my political leanings; worse, I don't want to belong" (79).

Tara is unable to come out of the traditional mould of an Indian woman in spite of her consciously adopted liberated attitude reflected in her acceptance of her son's gay sexuality and live-in relationship. Yet, despite all her efforts, she is unable to shake-off her Indianness. The American would not let her do that. Beth, an American women's welfare activist, thinks all Indians are alike and wants her to talk to another Indian, Nafisa's mother who she thinks has been beaten by her husband. In exasperation Tara cries out, "Nafisa's mother and I don't speak the same dialect. We don't even speak the language. I am tired of explaining India to Americans. I am sick of feeling an alien" (87).

In an interview with bookreporter.com, Mukherjee has remarked that she writes "in the tradition of immigrant experience rather than nostalgia and expatriation." However, Tara in *Desirable Daughters* is unable to completely restructure conventional gender roles. Nyman terms Tara's struggle as "a desire of constructing hybridity and forming new forms of identity and culture in space" (56).

Through her female protagonist, Mukherjee expresses her concern at the problem of assimilation of traditionality and spiritualism of East with materialism of the West. Commenting on this aspect in her novels Pushpa N. Parekh writes, "Fear, anger, pain, bitterness, confusion, silence, irony, humour as well as pathos underline her observations as she discovers for herself the undefined median between the preservation of old world and a simulation into the new one" (197).

Mukherjee's affinity to Indian soil and culture is rooted in her fiction. Hence, whatever claim she makes about her real identity being American, her approach to life and its problems is moored in her Indian upbringing. Nevertheless, through her characters she explores the ways in which many heritages are combined into a new singular bowl in this age of globalisation. In the process immersing themselves in the present and looking forward to the future, her characters have to discover for themselves the social, religious, historical and political forces that have shaped them.

For Mukherjee, the narrative becomes a site for multiple convergences of identities both conflictive and collaborative. Through her characters she forces an interrogation of a continuous and homogenous narrative gesturing at a real 'multicultural' ethnic and national identity that is not framed within or excluded from the dominant cultural discourse, dismantling the established boundaries between majority and minority cultures.

Mukherjee's representation of diaspora is an emancipatory narrative of self re-invention. She foregrounds the positive transformation of her characters as a result of immigration in her works. She is able to show the tensions that hold her characters while they undergo this transformation from one culture, people, identity or place to another new social, political, cultural and geographical milieu. She endows her characters with a resilient and enabling power, which helps them to face the spatial cultural and temporal disruptions and come out victorious. They go through a process of assimilation where, the different cultural and ethnic communities come together to form a new culture.

WORKS CITED

Gabriel, Sharmani Patricia. "Between Mosaic and Melting Pot." *Negotiating Multiculturalism and Cultural Citizenship in Bharati Mukherjee's Narratives of Diaspora. Postcolonial Text,* Vol. 1, No. 2, 2005.

Hancock, Geoffrey. "An Interview with Bharati Mukherjee." *Canadian Fiction Magazine* 59, 1987.

http://www.bookreporter.com/au.mukherjee.asp interview with Bharati Mukherjee dated 28 March, 2002.

Jope, Nyman. "Transnational Travel in Bharati Mukherjee's Desirable Daughters." *The Atlantic Literary Review,* Vol. 3, No. 4, Oct.-Dec. 2002.

Mukherjee, Bharati. *Desirable Daughters,* New Delhi: Rupa, 2002.

——. *Darkness.* New York: Fawcett Cress, 1985.

——. *American Dreamer.* Mother Jones Magazine, Jan/Feb. 1997.

Parekh, Pushpa N. "Telling Her Tale: Narrative Voice and Gender Roles in Bharati Mukherjee's *Jasmine.*" Emmanuel Nelson ed. *Bharati Mukherjee: Critical Perspectives.* New York: Garland Publishing, 1993.

Tradition and Transformation in Bharati Mukherjee's *Desirable Daughters*

6

Hemalatha K.

Diaspora writings reveal the interaction of traditional culture with the culture of an adopted alien land and bring about a transformation in the inherited tradition and culture of the immigrant. Bharati Mukherjee, a diasporic writer of Indian origin, tries to show "how fractured in terms of ethnicity, language, class and socio-economic level, the Indo-American group" (Mukherjee. Commonwealth Club, Online) settled in America is, in her novel *Desirable Daughters*.

Tara Lata Ganguly, the Tree Bride, passes on the baton of the genetic coding of the *Sanskara* of Indian Nationalism to Tara Lata Chatterjee, the narrator, who metamorphoses from a self-centered, indulgent woman to a socially awakened soul, wishing to dissociate from hyphenated American status, to a full-fledged American identity, ready to participate actively in the making of a New American culture, promising equality of status to all immigrants who have adopted it and fostering an American nationalism as it were.

Desirable Daughters is the story of three sisters of an orthodox, aristocratic Brahmin family, each, with a different relationship to the mother country. The narrator, Tara, is the ex-wife of a Bengali Brahmin bridegroom, who happens to achieve great success as a software professional in Atherton, California and is in constant pursuit of more material wealth. Unhappy with the patriarchal lifestyle of a husband who apparently neglects his family, she moves away to Upper Haight Area of San Francisco to lead an adventurous and sexually promiscuous life.

Tara's elder sister, Parvati, marries a man of her choice in India, after completing her education in US, and leads an affluent life of a corporate wife. Uncomplainingly, she attends to a continuous stream of in-laws, barging in and out of the house. She is quite certain that as long as her cook and house keeper do not desert her she can manage the household without physical breakdown.

The eldest daughter Padma lives in New Jersey with a man not quite up-to the standards of her father. She, who had to turn down movie offers as a young girl, is a small time media person, when she is on her own at New Jersey. She is business minded and arranges parties where she sells Indian jewellery and clothes. As a teenager she fell in love with a Christian boy and her parents did not consent to the marriage of the two; so out of that romance might be she had an issue. The whole story revolves around the mystery of whether there was a child and whether he was the same stranger who was stalking the family.

It is believed that these girls who hailed from an orthodox Brahmin family were the descendants of Tara Lata the "tree bride". Tara Lata was wedded to a tree, to save her from a life of humiliation after passing away of her groom because of a snake bite. Tara Lata lived up to the grand old age of seventy years, indulging in selfless service to all those who approached her for help. She lived in "a single house in an impoverished village...and gradually changed the world" (17). Bharati Mukherjee's comments that she was "unburdened by a time-consuming, emotion-draining marriage and children, never having to please a soul," (17) and so she was able to indulge in social and national service.

As a foil to her is Tara, the narrator, who married a man whom she had never met, her parent's choice. She was told that this was the best husband in the market. At this her teacher friends ask her, "how could any woman, even a nineteen-year-old, submit to someone else's choice, even a loving parent's? Obviously a recipe for disaster.... What do they know of the needs of a modern woman?" (26-27) In contrast to the tree bride who remained a virgin throughout life, Tara, the narrator, fickle mindedly divorces her husband and indulges in short-lived affairs with a live-in lover and other friends, in keeping with the customs of the place to which she has migrated. Towards the end of the novel, during a short reunion with her husband, she readily confesses:

> "Bish, *please*, it was *my* fault, *my* head was turned. I was so naïve, I had too much time and not enough to do" the whole silly mantra. He wouldn't listen. He would not permit collective guilt. Marriage is man's manifest dharma, his test, his duty, the outer sign of his inner strength and harmony. (265-66)

So may be if she had also indulged in some socially productive, commercially viable endeavour she would not have had so much free time and might have been less complaining and so would have succeeded in her wedding. Anyhow in this reunion, there is no longer the traditional belief of a husband being a "worshipful image of the morning" (7)—a God on whom the whole family depended.

Calcutta is the city which produced world famous playwrights, musicians and painters. It was described as the haven of "hope" and "to be a native born Calcutta was (and is) to be a Londoner, a Parisian, a New Yorker, at the zenith" (22). It was also believed that the elite or Bhadra Lok of Calcutta "share a tradition of leadership, of sensitivity, of achievement, refinement and beauty that was the envy of the world" (22). Contrary to such beliefs, Tara and her sister Padma have chosen to abandon their culture and adapt to the culture of the adopted land: "In America it seems to us, every woman was expected to create her own scandal, be the center of her own tangled love nest" (83).

The second generation, the son of the narrator, Rabi, also suffers because he develops homo-sexual tendencies and guilt complex as a consequence. The very language which Rabi spoke, his friendship with an impostor, a scoundrel, and his preference for a different sexual orientation are all second generation reactions to living in an open society where each one is free to choose his own morals.

Even Tara's sister in India, Parvati, could not understand why a young woman with everything she could ever want would ever decide to "leave her protector and provider" (66). Even though Tara wanted to return to India after her divorce, she was afraid it would not suit her son Rabi. The child who had been living in a big Atherton house earlier and studying with Silicon Valley kids had to shift to a smaller house at San Francisco and go to a private school which seemed more like an extended "playgroup than a learning environment" (66). Moreover, he who was not used to seeing his mother cry was now seeing her cry all the time.

Divorce and a paranoid existence with fear of impersonators and gangsters trying to fleece money out of the rich, elite and successful people made Tara feel incomplete, fractured and seek her live-in lover Andy's short-lived comforting assurances. Tara has reminiscences of a more stable lifestyle back home in India.

As a contrast to American youngsters, Indians didn't have outside influences like the media or lax schooling, or cars and dating and drugs. "We didn't know family breakdown... Our families existed inside an impenetrable bubble...no seeking after individual identity.... We were three sisters treated with absolute equality and we responded in total unanimity" (43-44).

Working as a school teacher, Tara is able to compare and contrast American school children with their Indian counterparts:

> Americans agonized and complained, they worked too hard for too little recognition, they got extensions, they slept through classes, they doped themselves up for tests, but Indians just did their work on time and did it better and reaped appropriate honors. Our training, not only in the old class rooms with second-rate equipments and uninspiring teachers, but also our training at home, duty and honor, obedience and respect, the whole dharma of studentship, spared us doubt and second thoughts. (44)

Bengali culture teaches one to claim the father's birthplace as one's own desh, one's home. Tara's American friends could not understand the fact that a Hindu Indian's last name announced his or her forefather's caste and place of origin. So

Tara tells them that they should be thankful for their "identity crises and feeling of alienation" (33). While in Bengal, Tara observes:

> Any community whose roots were not in Bengal, preferably in the eastern half of Bengal, anything like the Marwari, Parsi, or Sindhi community, was seen as alien and money-grubbing, worthy of our disrespect if not outright contempt. (214)

It is ironic that Tara's elder sister has to depend on Jagtiani, a Sindhi's generosity for sustenance while at New Jersey. Those whom we despise back home in India, become our companions when we emigrate to a multicultural society. This is the assertion of Mukherjee's belief that we have to "discourage the retention of cultural memory if the aim of that retention is cultural balkanization. We must think of American culture and nationhood as a constantly reforming, transmogrifying "we"" (Mukherjee. Motherjones Online).

In the novel even though there are nostalgic references to the past, her parental home, her forefathers' place of residence at Mishtigunj, she does not have an intense longing to go back home; instead she makes the best of a bad bargain; even though she is stalked by a murderer and is afraid of her son's future she does not plan to return permanently to India. As she herself has opined in an article:

> I have joined imaginative forces with an anonymous, driven, underclass of semi-assimilated Indians with sentimental attachments to a distant homeland but no real desire for permanent return. (Timothy 33)

At a certain point when she discusses her situation with her parents, she wonders that in case her sister was allowed to marry the Christian boy, then all this attack and her house being targetted for destruction might not have happened. Soon realization dawns on her, and she feels that instead of an attack by bombers, it may be an earthquake, plane crash or automobile accident. So there is no point questioning God's ways and what is needed is an acceptance of whatever is to happen and move forward in life.

As a school teacher, Tara experiences a oneness, a melting of identities and she feels totally assimilated and accepted when she is with little kids who are ninety per cent Asian, Latino and African-American and all other teachers European Americans. Here she declares that she is not "Asian".

> I am all things. When the little kids climb on my lap to be read to, or just listened to, I don't think they see me as anything different from their parents, the school nurse or their teachers. I thrive on this invisibility. It frees me to make myself over, by the hour. (78)

It would be interesting to know how she even canvassed for a gay Chicano candidate during the previous municipal elections. She does not want to be called Hindu, Brahmin, subcaste Kulin, Bengali from Calcutta whose region of ancestral origin is Mishtigunj.

> Playing with preschool children who teach me nursery rhymes in a language I don't speak or inside the book store on Haight Street where I immerse myself in heavy tomes on history of science or cosmology, I feel not just invisible, but heroically invisible, a border-crashing claimant of all people's legacies. (78-79)

Even though there are numerous references to fractured identities and failing relationships, at one point when Tara is with children there is a merging of identity and she does not feel "othered" but becomes invisible and this is what her writing seems to strive at.

During her short visit to India the book which her son picks up for her to read is about freedom fighters and in it there is a chapter, *The Betrayal and Death of Tara Ma,* Tara Lata Gangooly of Mishtigunj who had played an active role in the Quit India Movement in her own subtle way. On seeing this book, she feels that perhaps the Gods have sent them to her as a source of encouragement to her flagging spirits to rise up, fight and succeed in establishing an identity for herself as American, and not as hyphenated American. Mukherjee gives a clarion call to fellow immigrants to get actively involved in fighting discrimination and making their voice heard.

> If you are a citizen, let your vote count. Reinvest your energy and resources into revitalizing your city's disadvantaged residents and neighbourhoods. Know your constitutional rights, and when they are violated, use the agencies of redress the constitution makes available to you. (Mukherjee. Motherjones Online)

So Mukherjee is a determined writer focusing on asserting her rights and getting them implemented. She is angry when rights are violated and not afraid to voice her opinion to actively shape the future of her adopted homeland because she opines: "I celebrate racial and cultural mongrelization", (Mukherjee. Motherjones Online) and she declares:

> I am an American, not an Asian-American. My rejection of hyphenation has been called race treachery, but it is really a demand that America deliver the promises of its dreams to all its citizens equally. (Mukherjee. Motherjones Online)

WORKS CITED

Mukherjee, Bharati. www.commonwealthclub.org May 9, 2002.

——. *Desirable Daughters*. New Delhi: Rupa & Co., 2004.

——. www.motherjones.com, Jan./Feb. 1997 issue.

Timothy, Brennan. *Salman Rushdie and the Third World*. Great Britain: Macmillan Press.

Quest for Self and Immigrant Psyche in Bharati Mukherjee's *The Tiger's Daughter*

7

Ram Sharma

Bharati Mukherjee was born in 1940 in Calcutta. She married a Canadian fellow-student, Clark Blaise, at the University of Iowa, in 1963. She lived in Canada from 1966 to 1980. She became a naturalised Canadian, got Canadian citizenship and lived in Toronto and then in Montreal and held teaching positions at McGill University and Concordia University. She migrated to the U.S.A. in 1980 with her family and became a U.S.A. citizen in 1988. Her remarkable fictional works are *The Tiger's Daughter* (1972), *Wife* (1975), *Days and Nights in Calcutta (essays) Darkness* (1985), *The Middleman and other Stories* (1988). *The Sorrow and the Terror* (1987), *Jasmine* (1989), *The Holder of the World* (1993), *Leave It to Me* (1997) and *Desirable Daughters* (2002). Bharati Mukherjee's novels and short stories often reveal contemporary themes and concerns. One of these is the emotional and psychic consequences of search for self and immigrant psyche. Bharati Mukherjee in a recent interview has clearly stated her aim in her novels.

"We immigrants have fascinating tales to relate. Many of us have lived in newly independent or emerging countries which are placed by civil and religious conflicts.... When we uproot ourselves from those countries and come here, either by choice or out of necessity, we suddenly must know about 200 years of American history and learn to adopt to American society. I attempt to illustrate this in my novels and short stories. My aim is to explore Americans to the energetic voices of new settlers in this country" (Interview). When a person visits the unknown land, he is an outsider in a no man's land and there he has to struggle a lot for his survival, conquering these new feelings of nostalgia. He carves out a new territory and wraps himself totally with the lure of the West. He recreates himself into a new personality and forms emotional ties with the place he lives in. This discovery of a new self slowly makes him forget his own native culture. When he returns to his native land he finds that his native taste and touch have turned alien to him. His mind is again torn apart between the cultural clash of two environments and split personality.

Same is the story with Tara in *The Tiger's Daughter* who comes across a similar kind of bewilderment on her visit to India after seven years. The protagonist named Tara Banerjee Cartwright is an autobiographical presentation of the author herself who is also married to an American. In her Canadian Fiction Magazine interview, Mukherjee mentions that *The Tiger's Daughter* was "written on a summer break in response to a request" from an editor from Houghton Mifflin who had been impressed by a story she had published in Massachusetts Review. The Tiger's Daughter is Tara Banerjee, a Bengali Brahmin of Calcutta and daughter of an industrialist known as Bengal Tiger, schooled at Pough Keepsie, New York and married to an American named David who is a writer. After her marriage Tara becomes Tara Banerjee Cartwright. The protagonist's habit of retaining her maiden surname after marriage symbolically reflects her subconscious mind which is still deeply rooted in her native land and she actually has not been able to forget it in spite of the changed identity of a European, adopted by her. There is a strange fusion of the Americanness and Indianness in the psyche of Tara and they are always at a note of confrontation with each other. Tara Banerjee Cartwright makes a trip to India after being there for seven years. When she visits India, "the alien Western culture which has almost become a second self to her is constantly in clash with the culture of the native soil" (Barat 54). Tara finds it difficult to adjust with her friends and relatives in India, and sometimes with the traditions of her own family. She feels loneliness in her own native land. Tara expected that her return to India would remove her displeasure of staying abroad which is described in the following lines:

> For years she had dreamed of this return to India. She had believed that all hesitations, all shadowy fears of the time abroad would be erased quite magically if she could just return home to Calcutta. But so far the return had brought only wounds. First the corrosive hours on Marine Drive, then the deformed beggar in the Railway station, and now the inexorable train ride steadily undid what strength she had held in reserve. She was an embittered woman, she now thought, old and cynical at twenty-two and quick to take offence. (25)

Her first stepping on the land of India at Bombay fills her with disappointment. It seems that the alien land has become more of a home to her. She repents to have come to India without her husband and she is unable to keep him off her mind. "Perhaps I was stupid to come without him, she thought, even with him rewriting his novel during the vacation. Perhaps I was too impulsive, confusing my fear of New York with homesickness. Or perhaps I was going mad" (21). Alam observes,

> Tara's journey from Bombay to Calcutta brings an equally disgusting experience to her. She feels that Calcutta too has changed and deteriorated. She finds Calcutta in the grip of violence due to riots, caused by the confrontation between different classes of society. Her changed personality makes her misfit in the company of her friends and relatives and makes her unable to participate in the ritual functions of home. Tara also feels that her mother's attitude towards her has changed and she too appears to be unhappy at her marriage. (Alam 37)

The author comments,

> Perhaps her mother, sitting severely before God on a tiny rug, no longer loved her either. After all Tara had wilfully abandoned her caste by marrying a foreigner. Perhaps her mother was offended that she, no longer a real Brahmin, was constantly in and out of this sacred room, dipping like a crow. (50)

The most important cause aggravating her discomfort and unease is her marriage which hangs on her heart as a burden:

> In India she felt she was not married to a person but to a foreigner and this foreignness was a burden. It was hard for her to talk about marriage responsibilities in Camac Street; her friends were curious only about the adjustments she has made. (62)

Tara is bogged down by two personalities one of an Indian and the other of an American. During such critical moments she felt that she should go back to her husband David because she feels that she would be more at ease there. Tara also feels that she has forgotten many of her Hindu rituals of worshipping icons which she had seen her mother performing since her childhood:

> When the sandal wood paste had been ground Tara scraped it off the slimy tablet with her fingers and poured it into a small silver bowl. But she could not remember the next step of the ritual. It was not a simple loss. Tara feared this forgetting of prescribed actions; it was a little death, a hardening of the heart, a cracking of axis and center. But her mother came quickly with the relief of words. (51)

The phrase 'cracking of axis and center' symbolically points out the psyche of Tara which has come in her due to the loss of her own cultural heritage (Bharat 56). There are several other instances in the text which illustrate her loss of cultural heritage:

> And sad, Tara thought, in spite of the promised *bhajan*. As a child, Tara remembered, she had sung *bhajans* in that house. She had sat on a love seat beside a very holy man with a limp and had sung *Raghupati Raghava Rajaram*. But that had been a very long time ago, before some invisible spirit on darkness had covered her like skin. (54)

Tara's negative reaction at the changed social situation and deterioration of Calcutta makes her friend Reena to comment about her that she has "become too self-centered and European" (105).

Tara makes Reena realize that the life of Calcutta, in spite of all the dark spots and drawbacks, has its own life which is found nowhere else and which her husband David would not be able to realize in spite of his vision and knowledge of India through books.

> She thought about Calcutta. Not of the poor sleeping on main streets, dying on obscure thoroughfares. But of the consolation Calcutta offers. Life can be very pleasant here, thought Tara. (132)

Tara also provides a comparative picture of New York and Calcutta. "Tara told him how much easier she thought it was to live in Calcutta. How much simpler to trust the city's police inspector and play tennis with him on Saturdays. How humane to accompany a friendly editor to watch the riots in town. New York, she confided, was a gruesome nightmare. It wasn't muggings she feared so much as rude little invasions" (69).

Tara also feels that the Indians who are crazy of foreign things, dress and items do not approve marriage with foreign people.

> They were racial purists, thought Tara desperately. They liked foreigners in movie magazines—Nat Wood and Bob Wagner in faded *Photoplays*. They loved Englishmen like Worthington at the British Council. But they did not approve of foreign marriage patterns. So much for the glamour of her own marriage. She had expected admiration from these friends. She had wanted them to consider her marriage an emancipated gesture. But emancipation was suspicious—it presupported bondage. (86)

"Tara feels herself, as misfit everywhere she goes. She is forced to look at her inner world consisting of two cultures and the two different ideologies which are two worlds wide apart. Realizing that the reconciliation is impossible, Tara feels to go back to David" (Lal 112). Her father Bengal Tiger in order to entertain her plans their short stay at Darjeeling to spend the summer but Tara gets no consolation anywhere. She goes to Air

India office and reserves a seat on a flight to New York. Her journey is decided but after a short interval of this reservation Tara becomes a victim of violence, caused by the marchers who were proceeding towards the Catelli-continental in a mob. The end of Tara remains mysterious and there is a suggestion that Tara does not survive in the violence of the mob which does not even spare the old man Joyonto Roy Choudhury. Locked in the car, Tara only thinks about her husband David. This novel ends with these lines "And Tara, still locked in a car across the street from the Catelli-continental, wondered whether she would even get out of Calcutta, and if she didn't whether David would even know that she loved him fiercely" (210).

It is in India that Tara feels dislocated and displaced. In this way, Tara's journey to India proves as a quest for self and her immigrant psyche which proves frustrating, slowly leads her to illusion, alienation, depression and finally to her tragic end.

WORKS CITED

Alam, Fakrul. *Bharati Mukherjee.* New York: Twayane Publishers, 1996.

Barat, Anand Prabha. "Bharati Mukherjee and the Immigrant Psyche: The Tiger's Daughter." *The Fiction of Bharati Mukherjee: A Critical Symposium.* R.K. Dhawan (Ed.). New Delhi: Prestige Books, 1996.

"Interview." Quoted in Sunday Review, *The Times of India.* Oct. 1, 1989.

Lal, Malashiri. *The Law of the Threshold.* Shimla: Indian Institute of Advance Studies, 1995.

Mukherjee, Bharati. *The Tiger's Daughter.* First published by Houghton Mifflin Company, 1971, Published in Penguin Books, 1987. Reissued by Penguin Books India, 1990.

Dimple's Neurotic Behaviour in Bharati Mukherjee's *Wife*

8

Archana Trivedi

The term neurosis has become a part of our everyday vocabulary. To say, "He is neurotic", can be anything from a complaint about someone whose behavior is consistently annoying, to a term of sympathy for someone who is frequently distressed and is somehow unable to work or relate effectively. The concept of neurosis as a type of emotional disturbance was popularized by Freud. He viewed neurosis as a pattern of behavioral and psychological disturbance produced by conflict within the personality structure. From this perspective, neurosis is a relatively specific disorder. Consequently, neurotic individuals experience acute distress, and engage in a variety of behaviors designed to avoid or reduce the distress. These behaviors of avoidance frequently interfere with everyday functioning. Thus, the neurotic might be unable to relate well to others.

At this time Freud's thoughts became more and more sociologically-oriented. Freud had highly qualified belief in the essential good nature of human beings. He held that people group together primarily to satisfy their needs which is not possible in isolation and common hatred can unite them in love. This view cannot be easily dismissed because there is no concrete scientific evidence to prove that human beings are either good or bad by nature. Men are, therefore, perpetually on the look out for pleasure and long for the absence of misery. The purpose of life is decided by the "programme of the pleasure principle" (Freud 163). But all the 'regulations of the universe' embodied by civilization "run counter to it". Man has to grapple with at least three important sources of suffering—from his own body, from the external world and from human relationships. The last of these is artificial and avoidable but the most painful at the same time. As a natural reaction to this, man may seek refuge in voluntary isolation (the extreme form being the annihilation of all instincts), sublimate his instincts (and get a qualified satisfaction), or create an alternate delusional world where the ugly and unpleasant features of reality find no place.

Indian English women novelists have favorably responded to the changed psychological realities of Indian life after independence and give an authentic treatment to this situation. An interesting preoccupation of these writers appear to be delving into the labyrinthine depths of the Indian psyche and showing its relation to society. And nowhere is this concern more obvious than in the novels that figure neurotic characters. The characters are shown as grappling on the one hand with the changed realities of Indian life and the trauma they entail and on the other hand with the psychic conflicts of personal origin. These conflicts and traumas become too pronounced at a particular point of time in their life and their ability to hold their feelings under repression gives ways. Anita Desai's *Cry, The Peacock* and *Where shall We Go This Summer?*, Kamala Markandaya's *A Silence of Desire,* Shashi Deshpande's *That Long Silence,* Ruth Prawer Jhabvala's *Get Ready for Battle,* Nayantara Sahgal's *The Day in Shadow,* Nergis Dalal's *The Inner Door* and Bharati Mukherjee's *Wife,* portray sensitive individuals in their moments of intense struggle and in their efforts to seek neurotic solutions to their problems. In the course of the ordeal the protagonists of these novels find themselves at odds with society and undergo various degrees of psychological transformation. Both as a physical reality outside and a psychic agent within, society which we take to mean the essence of one's relationships with others plays a very important role.

The study of these novelists, especially for the study of neurotic characters, highlights another important theme that has been frequently harped upon is the cultural conflict resulting from a character's exposure to a different culture. Again, the extent of cultural shock depends on the individual's susceptibility and the psychic conflicts he carries in his unconsciousness.

Bharati Mukherjee's *Wife* is often chosen to demonstrate what devastation a hostile culture can cause in a sensitive individual (Parenthetically it may be observed that neurosis is known to occur more frequently among immigrant population).

A study of *Wife* shows Dimple in an entirely new light. The already existing neurotic picture in her is precipitated and aggravated by her American life. Her husband does not suffer from any of those conflicts because his psyche is structured entirely differently. What then ultimately interests us is not so much the cultural conflict but the psychological suffering of the individual to which the cultural conflicts often contribute.

Bharati Mukherjee's novel *Wife* stands out as a unique fictional work by virtue of its insightful probing into its heroine's psyche. *Wife* is the simple story of Amit and his wife Dimple, newly married Bengali immigrants to the U.S.A. Dimple's ill-concealed compulsions are soon precipitated by the violence ridden and individualistic American life and culminate in her killing of her husband. This psychic development in Dimple has been variously but uncritically viewed as her desperate efforts to "forget" her Indian roots are necessitated by the demands of American life and her assertion of independence from her overbearing husband. In this light it can be argued that Dimple suffers from the neurotic compulsion of indulging in abnormal acts in order to conceal her own sense of intrinsic weakness and failure.

Bharati Mukherjee's *Wife* falls into the category of the modern novel as it presents an intense inner world of neurotic and solipsistic individual. Instead of trying to combine the freedom of the individual with tolerance for fellow beings, Bharati Mukherjee chooses to glorify the alienated individual. Rootlessness and unreal existence are the main concerns of this expatriate novelist who has set out to make a deliberate distortion of Indian womanhood. Her women characters are tantalized by the possibility of passion, which they mistake for love and self-expression. America which appears to be a free land, a veritable dreamland is the enigma of existence for all Indian girls.

Dimple, the protagonist in *Wife* is an extremely immature girl who constantly dreams of marriage as she hopes that it would bring freedom and love. At the same time she is not clear about the concepts of freedom and love. This ambiguity underlying her mental make up defines the incompleteness of her very being. After a painful waiting which makes her desperate and suicidal, Dimple Das Gupta, the pliant, docile, obedient and submissive daughter of a middle class Bengali family marries Amit Basu, an ambitious engineer, chosen by her parents, about to migrate to the U.S. "She thought of pre-marital life as dress rehearsal for actual living" (3). Delay in marriage has made her very nervous and anxious so when she is married ostensibly to a worthy groom by Indian standards of marriage, her chances of happiness ought to be very high.

But soon after her marriage, she feels cheated as her romantic, adolescent mind cannot grasp the reality that freedom too has certain limitations. Her husband, Amit Kumar Basu, is an average middle class, unimaginative, young engineer who dreams of making a fortune in America and on retiring to live a comfortable rich life in Calcutta. She begins to resent her new home, her in-laws and even her husband who does not seem to be capable of feeding her fantasy. Amit fails to meet out the requirements of her imaginative world. She does not like the new name 'Nandini', given to her by her mother-in-law, she finds the apartment very small, unattractive; the sight of the wounded crow is exceedingly loathsome to her, but at this stage it is a passive resistance only: "it was this passive resistance, this withholding of niggardly affection from Amit, this burying of one's head among dusty, lace doilies that she found so degrading" (30). At this stage, when she begins to reconstruct her 'ideal' man, on the basis of the faces from magazines, and is unable to identify herself with anyone in the family, the prospect of becoming a mother enrages her. She treats it as an outrage on her body and induces an abortion, disposing of that "tyrannical and vile" thing deposited in her body. She justifies herself by arguing that she cannot afford to take any relics from her old life to America where she hopes to begin life afresh and become a more exciting person. Dimple has lived so long in a fantasy world of advertising and advice columns that she is emotionally incapable of understanding another human being, as she cannot understand Amit.

Dimple's vision of Sita's docility, sacrifice and responsibility is a flag with many messages. She wants to break through the traditional taboos of a wife. She aspires for freedom and love in marriage. This aim brings her indignation, grief, resentment, peevishness, spite and sterile anger. Dimple wants to do away with traditional taboos of a wife and hence she becomes an escapist, lost in her world of fantasy. In the U.S. she thinks of herself as some kind of non-human being like a bug. She feels as if she is instinctively drawn towards some disastrous end: "It was as if some force was impelling her towards disaster; some monster had overtaken her body, a creature with serpentine curls and heaving bosom that would erupt indiscreetly through one of Dimple's orifices, leaving her, Dimple Basu, splattered like a bug on the living room wall and rug" (156).

Once again, even after going to America, her hopes are belied. She tries hard to adjust to Amit's wishes and be dutiful wife, she is never quite unaware of the fact that he is not the man of her dreams. Life with him, both in India and America, is naturally a big disappointment for her. Marriage has not "provided all the glittery things she had imagined had not brought her cocktails under canopied skies" (101). Like any traditionally brought up Indian husband, Amit does not know how to pay a compliment to his wife. He would like her to stay at home and attend to the household chores rather than go out, work and earn. In a word, he appears to be almost a personification of *Ego* in the Freudian sense.

Amit fails Dimple on all planes—physical, mental and emotional "on her very first day in the H.Y.V. apartment she felt like a star collapsing inwardly" (69). She tries to convey her fears and forebodings to Amit but neither does he try to understand her nor is he capable of rising above a mundane understanding. Dimple's psychological imbalances, her immoderate daytime sleeping, her nightmares, her indecisiveness—everything remains unknown to him up to his dying day.

Dimple has to cope up with her traumatic mental condition all alone. "She had expected pain when she had come to America, had told herself that pain was part of any new beginning, and the sweet structures of that new life had allotted pain a special place" (109). She is shaken by the knowledge that America with all its outward glitter allows Indian wives only to create "little Indians" around them but does not allow them either freedom or fulfillment as evident in the case of Ina Mullick who, despite her attempts at becoming 'a total American', remains a frustrated individual. After this disturbing realization, Dimple sinks into a world of isolation, unable to welcome the bright prospect of setting up a new home even after Amit gets a job. She turns towards Ina, Leni and ultimately Milt Glasser in her moments of crises. Ina and Leni fail her as friends. After a few pathetic attempts to merge herself into the new culture by wearing the borrowed outfit of Marsha and by flirting with Milt Glasser, Dimple experiences total estrangement from herself and her surroundings as well. Torn by the conflict between her fantasy world and the reality of her situation, she allows her mind to be totally conditioned by the commercials on T.V. and magazines so much so she loses the ability to distinguish them from the world of reality. She is caught in a whirlwind of traumatic emotions—her tradition questioning her outrageous adultery and her present confused self-wishing to become American by any means. "I am terrible in crises" (204) she had told Meena and she is true to her words in the moments of her crisis. Her extra-marital affair gives rise to a growing feeling of guilt. Given the right opportunity, she might have confided in Amit but Amit's inactiveness blocks the outlay. Torn by her psychic and emotional tensions, she takes the drastic step of murdering her husband thinking that she cannot bear this sort of life forever. In a stunningly calm and cool manner she takes out the knife from the kitchen drawer and drives it down on a spot near his hairline repeatedly hitting at the same place seven times. Thus she punishes her inattentive husband for his lapses and unceremoniously ends up her disharmonious marital life. Finally, she kills Amit to suppress her guilty conscience and also to feel very American, almost like a character in a T.V. serial.

In *Wife* Bharati Mukherjee had portrayed the enigma of existence, the hollowness of the Indian institutionalized marriage. Bharati Mukherjee had seen the stereotypical pattern of conventional Indian marriage. Being the writer of modern time, she has depicted in her fiction the problems faced by Indian and other Third-World immigrants who attempt to assimilate into North American lifestyles. Mukherjee focuses upon sensitive protagonists who lack a stable sense of personal and cultural identity and are victimized by racism, sexism and other forms of social oppression.

In an interview with Moline Bharati Mukherjee has clearly stated her aim in her writings. "We immigrants have fascinating tales to relate. Many of us have lived in newly independent or emerging countries. When we uproot ourselves from those countries and come here, either by choice or out of necessity, we suddenly must absorb 200 years of American society. I attempt to illustrate this in my novels and stories. My aim is to expose Americans to the energetic voices of new settles in this country" (219). In fact Mukherjee had come to terms with her own identity in an alien land, caught as she was between two conflicting cultures. Also, she had to contend with racial discrimination during the years she spent in Canada, precisely between 1972 and 1980. She managed to overcome both the crises and this brought her a sense of elevation and confidence. Mukherjee's early experiences had a great bearing on her writing and outlook of life.

In *Wife,* Dimple is trapped between two cultures, and aspires to a third, imagined world. Living in her social vacuum, Dimple is not unlike hundreds of American men and women who believe and are betrayed by the promise of fulfillment offered by the media, and who choose the solution suggested by a violent environment. Violence is her fundamental experience of New York and thus despair sets in her life. She thinks "her own body seemed curiously alien to her, filled with hate, malice an instance desire to hurt, yet weightless, almost airborne" (117). Television introduces her to love, middle-American style. Her T.V. watching stuns her by the incredible violence. It becomes a diabolical trap, a torment without hope of either release or relief. Dimple has been portrayed free and rebelling throughout the novel. She has no inhibition in expressing whatever she feels. The murder of Amit is an assertion of her American identity. The novel traces the enigma of existence, the psychic breakdown of an Indian wife in America. She is neither of India nor of America but a stunned wanderer between these two worlds, yet is trying to attain a distinct identity. Neither does she belong to the T.V. world nor to the world of reality but keeps on shuttling between the two. She is yet to release her 'self' from the hallucinatory world, she is yet to get out of her schizophrenic self. A waylaid traveler, she is yet to reach her destination and carve out a niche for herself.

WORKS CITED

Freud, Sigmund. *Civilization and its Discontents.* Harmondsworth: Penguin, 1964.

Interview with Karen Moline, Australia: Harper's Bazaar, Autumn 1990.

Mukherjee, Bharati. *Wife.* India: Penguin Books, 1990.

Between Two Worlds: Jhumpa Lahiri's *Interpreter of Maladies*

9

A.N. Dwivedi

Dedicated to the author's parents and sister, *Interpreter of Maladies* (published in 1999) is Jhumpa Lahiri's well-known collection of short stories which won for her the coveted Pulitzer Prize for Fiction in 2000. This collection was her first venture in imaginative literature, full of suspense and surprise, melancholy and mystery. It consists of nine dazzling stories *in toto,* and these stories narrate the lives of Indians settled in America, of people "navigating between the strict traditions they've inherited and the baffling New World they must encounter every day" (cited from the inner flap of *Interpreter of Maladies*: 1999). The cross-cultural contact is so conspicuous in it, and the old and new worlds inevitably coalesce herein to suggest the birth of a fresh world-order.

The first story in *Interpreter of Maladies* is "A Temporary Matter", which deals with the estrangement of Shukumar, aged 35, and his wife Shoba, now 33. Shukumar is still busy in his research work on "agrarian revolts in India" (2). He has no employment on hand, leaving the burden of house-running to his wife, who does the job of a proof-reader of textbooks. Her office-compulsions compel her to stay late at work and her outings with Gillian make Shukumar jealous and restless. She even thinks of having a separate apartment for herself. The rostering of electricity in the city of Boston for five days creates a situation for the couple in which they are willy-nilly dragged into conversation with each other. They have to fill-up the period of darkness with tales of their own. Through a little poem, a joke or a fact about the world surrounding them, they break the silence. Shoba, who is presently pregnant, gives birth to a 'dead baby' in a local hospital. Unto the last, Shoba keeps the gender of the baby a secret in order to surprise her husband, but Shukumar knows it because he had held the baby in his hands before it was cremated: "Our baby was a boy" (22). The couple grieve over it, and the shared grief unites them unexpectedly.

"When Mr. Pirzada Came to Dine" relates the story of Pirzada, who has a three storey house in Dacca, a Lecturership in Botany at the University, a wife of twenty years, and seven daughters between the ages of six and sixteen. That was the time of Civil War (in 1971) when Sheikh Mujibur Rahman was leading Bangladesh for freedom from the clutches of Pakistan. Mr. Pirzada, who always sets his watch to Dacca time, is worried about his family in Dacca. He is on a visit to America and has been awarded a grant from the government of Pakistan to study the foliage of New England. As his grant is frugal, he has to live in a room in a graduate dormitory and does not have "a proper stove or a television set of his own" (24). So, he comes to the narrator's house to gather news about the life or death of his family. Being a Bengali Muslim, Mr. Pirzada is always worried about the safety of his wife and daughters during the Indo-Pak war. The war ends with the creation of Bangladesh as a new nation: "Of course, was outdated by then" (41). In January 1972, he flew back to Dacca and found, luckily, the family safe. The short letter from Mr. Pirzada to this effect gladdens the narrator and the parents.

The third story, "Interpreter of Maladies" (which gives title to the collection of short stories) introduces Mr. and Mrs. Das, with their three children—Tina (daughter), Ronny and Bobby (sons)—on a visit to India from America. The Das family "looked Indian but dressed as foreigners did" (43-44), is being guided by Mr. Kapasi in its tour to the Sun Temple at Konark. Mr. and Mrs. Das are very young, perhaps not even thirty, and their children are frolicsome and jolly. On the way, Mr. Kapasi tells Mr. Das that he guides tours only on Fridays and Saturdays, and that he has "another job during the week" (50). On other days, he works as an interpreter for a doctor. "He [the doctor] has a number of Gujarati patients. My father was

Gujarati, but many people do not speak Gujarati in this area, including the doctor. And so the doctor asked me to work in his office, interpreting what the patients say" (50). And Mr. Kapasi knows English too. Mrs. Das is now interested in the job of Mr. Kapasi and calls it 'romantic' and one of 'a big responsibility'. Mr. Das also agrees with her. But to Mr. Kapasi, it is "a thankless occupation" and "nothing noble in interpreting people's maladies, assiduously translating the symptoms of so many swollen bones, countless cramps of bellies and bowels, spots on people's palms that changed color, shape, or size" (51). Initially, he had dreamed of being an interpreter for diplomats and dignitaries, but that could not be. Once his son contracted typhoid and he had to pay the increasingly exorbitant medical bills. Though his son died one evening in his mother's arms, he had no money to pay for the funeral or for the other children's schooling. So, he became an interpreter of maladies to earn more money and also to save other children's lives. But his wife "had little regard for his career as an interpreter" (53). As an interpreter, however, Mr. Kapasi intoxicates Mrs. Das when he tells her about a number of patients and their diseases. Also, the Konark temple engravings arouse her romantic feelings. Any woman can blush to see them—"the countless friezes of entwined naked bodies, making love in various positions, women clinging to the necks of men, their knees wrapped eternally around their lovers' thighs" (57). Mr. Kapasi is also drawn towards Mrs. Das, and when she demands his address to send the copies of photos he readily gives it to her on a scrap of paper. He starts admiring her legs and bare limbs, and wishes "to be alone with her" (58). And when such a situation arises, Mrs. Das makes a startling revelation to Mr. Kapasi—that Bobby is not Raj's son. She has kept it "a secret for eight whole years" (62). After this confession, she feels a great relief, though the sense of guilt overpowers her wherever she goes.

The fourth story, "A Real Durwan", deals with Boori Ma, sweeper of the stairwell and protector of a three-floor flat. Boori Ma is aged 64 and is a victim of Partition. She is now separated from her husband, four daughters, two storey house, a rosewood *almari* and a number of coffer boxes. She still carries a bunch of skeleton keys and her life savings, tied to the free end of her *sari*. She is a dreamy woman, talking ever of her previous comforts when she "worked as hired help for a prosperous *zamindar* back east" (73). Presently, she is a poor creature, carrying her reed broom wherever she goes, and patrols the activities in the alley, screens the itinerant pedlars selling combs and shawls, calls a rickshaw for residents and routs any suspicious character with her broom. Consequently, she is regarded as "a real durwan" (73). She is fond of saying time and again "Believe me, don't believe me...". Mr. and Mrs. Dalal promise to replace her tattered quilts before they leave for Shimla, and she has no bed but only newspapers to sleep on. Meanwhile, she has shifted from the stairwell to the rooftop for her shelter, as the stairwell undergoes renovation. On the rooftop, there is no one to talk to, and so Boori Ma becomes restless. She wanders through the markets for some exercise and starts spending "her life savings on small treats" (81). She loses the rest of her life savings and skeleton keys in the busy market place. When she returns, the residents of the flat start accusing her of neglecting her duty—the new basin fixed on the stairwell has been stolen, and a big hole is seen in the whitewashed wall, and a tangle of rubber tubes and pipes is sticking out of it. The residents cry aloud: "This is all her doing", and "For days she has been wandering the streets, speaking to strangers" (81). Boori Ma is eventually thrown out with her belongings, and the residents search for a real *durwan*.

The fifth story, "Sexy", is about Miranda, a young Midwestern woman, falling in love with a married Bengali man called Devajit Mitra (shortened to Dev). The wife of Dev has gone to India along with her son, Rohin. She is Laxmi's cousin, whose husband (Dev) is attracted by the charms of Miranda. Dev and Miranda pass together many hours on Sundays and make intense love to each other. Once on an outing with Miranda to the Mapparium at the Christian Science Centre, he impulsively calls her 'sexy': "You're sexy" (91). Then the news comes that Dev's wife and son are returning from India soon at the invitation of Laxmi. They arrive soon after and Laxmi and her cousin visit a beauty saloon. When the boy and Miranda are left alone, they become friendly, play the game of 'the country and the capital', and take tea together. He urges her to put on her cocktail dress, and when she has adorned herself in this dress he calls her 'sexy'. She is utterly surprised to hear this word and asks him its meaning. He replies: "It means loving someone you don't know" (107). He informs her that his father had loved "someone sexy" and that "now he loves her instead of my mother" (108). She presently realizes, through cries and sobs, that Rohin is Dev's son and his wife Rohin's mother. The story is a bit longer than other stories in this volume, but the plot-structure is thin.

"Mrs. Sen" is the sixth story in this collection, dealing with the nervousness of Mrs. Sen in learning how to drive in order to keep her job of supervising a boy of eleven years called Eliot after school. Mrs. Sen is the wife of Mr. Sen who teaches Mathematics at the university. She has plenty of time at home, and hence she becomes a child caretaker. In due course, Eliot comes to know that there are two things which make Mrs. Sen happy: one, the arrival of a letter from her family, and two, fish from the seaside (121-23). But what worries her most is the skill of driving, which she fails to master due to confusion and lack of confidence. Once when driving the car, she collides with a telephone pole, but luckily she as well as Eliot escapes unhurt. The policeman, who arrives to inquire into the accident, lets her go with her husband, saying "Very lucky to come out without a scratch" (134). Thereafter, Mrs. Sen gives up her job of a baby sitter.

The next story, "This Blessed House", is about a young couple—Sanjeev and Twinkle. Though Sanjeev keeps reminding his wife that "... we're not Christian. We're good little Hindus" (137, 146), Twinkle has a natural inclination towards collecting "Christian paraphernalia" (137), including the statue of unbearded Jesus kept on top of the fireplace mantel, a 3-D postcard of Saint Francis done in four colours, three bedrooms decorated with scenes from the Bible, etc. Sanjeev has graduated in engineering from MIT and is presently working for a firm near Hartford. Aged 33, he has a secretary of his own and a dozen people working under his supervision. His wife, Twinkle, is completing her master's thesis at Stanford on an Irish poet. The couple arrange a wedding party in a house in the neighbourhood. One day while strolling on the lawn, Twinkle shrieks suddenly on seeing a plaster Virgin Mary behind an overgrown bush. She is immensely attracted towards the statue and wants to place it on the front lawn so that every passer-by looks at it, but Sanjeev does not like the idea and desires to put it in the garage. Twinkle reminds him that 'the blessed house' belongs to both and that she won't allow him to dump it. By way of a compromise, they decide to place the statue in a recess at the side of the house where it could be seen by guests visiting them. The guests arrive for the party and are greeted with gin and beer in the midst of deafening music. Twinkle invites them all to explore the attic where they reach by means of a ladder. There they sing and dance and cry aloud in merry-making. When they come down, Twinkle is seen holding "a solid silver bust of Christ" (156). This irks Sanjeev terribly: "Most of all he hated it because he knew that Twinkle loved it" (157). Willy-nilly, he holds the silver bust in his hands and follows her quietly.

The eighth story, "The Treatment of Bibi Haldar", is about a strange malady Bibi Haldar is suffering from. All efforts to treat her prove abortive. Consultations with allopaths, homeopaths and ayurvedics have yielded no tangible results. Her paroxysm creates hypertensions and physical convulsions in her. She becomes somewhat relieved when she hears from a well-meaning doctor that "relations will calm her blood" (162). Her only relations are an elderly cousin and his wife, who keep her isolated in the storage room. But by 'relations' the doctor clearly means "a man" (160), "a husband" (163). The question is how to get a man for an insane woman? Mr. Haldar and his wife are not favourably inclined to the idea of marriage, but on the persuasion of neighbours, Mr. Haldar places a one-line advertisement in the town newspaper for it. To the exasperation of all, no man responds to the advertisement. Meanwhile, Mr. Haldar's wife becomes pregnant and in due course delivers a girl. With the birth of this girl, Mr. Haldar and wife totally distance themselves from Bibi Haldar, and later go away, leaving Bibi to the hazards of the strange world. The narrator informs us, at the close of the story, that Bibi gets disgraced by someone in her loneliness and under the supervision of neighbours delivers a son. Now, Bibi stands "cured" (172).

The ninth and last short story, "The Third and Final Continent", recounts a Bengali youngman's departure for England, where he stays for some time and then shifts to America to accept a full-time job in the library at M.I.T. Hence his salary is "generous enough to support a wife" (174). He obtains a green card, besides being contented to be hired by a world-famous university. He hires an eight-dollar room per week for himself in Mrs. Croft's house, and resides there for six weeks only. He comes to know from Mrs. Croft's daughter, Helen, that the old lady is aged 103. Then his wife Mala arrives in America, and he shifts to a furnished apartment on the M.I.T. campus. He once takes his wife to Mrs. Croft's house and introduces her to the old lady. Mrs. Croft finds her "a perfect lady" (195). Later on, Mrs. Croft dies a lonely death, rendering the Bengali narrator a sad and dejected man. Meanwhile, a son is born to the Bengali couple, and on growing up the son attends the Harvard University. He is a promising youngman who generates high hopes in his parents. His father thinks of him thus: "...if I can survive on three continents, then there is no obstacle he cannot conquer" (197-98). Obviously, the story ends on a note of optimism and wishful flight of fancy.

In *Interpreter of Maladies,* Jhumpa Lahiri apparently hovers between two worlds—the East and the West. Accordingly, most of her characters, both male and female, display a sort of attitudinal conflict in their response to various situations in life. They are mostly Indians living in fast-moving America: Shukumar and his wife Shoba finding it difficult to reside under the same roof; Mr. Pirzada ever thinking about his wife and daughters stationed in the war-torn Bangladesh; Mr. Das and Mrs. Das presently visiting India and Mrs. Das's revelation of her rape by a robust Sardar whose son Bobby is; the romantic role of Mr. Kapasi as a tour guide for the Das family reminding us of R.K. Narayan's Raju in *The Guide* (1958), and serving as an 'interpreter of maladies' in a doctor's clinic for five days per week to meet his family expenses; Dev and Miranda (a Midwestern woman) making intense love to each other; Mrs. Sen keenly desiring to learn to drive in order to save her job of looking after the boy Eliot; Sanjeev and Twinkle ever anxious to keep their house 'blessed'; Bibi Haldar suffering from a psychological problem of getting a suitable husband for herself; and the Bengali youngman going to England and then to the United States in search of an employment and his acquaintance with a centurian, Mrs. Croft, who provides him rented residence initially. Obviously, these different characters are drawn from both India and America and largely belong to middle-class families struggling for prosperity and position. More often than not, they are caught between the two diametrically opposed worlds, and their tension and restlessness add a peculiar artistic charm to this collection of short stories.

To conclude, *Interpreter of Maladies* clearly demonstrates the expatriate sensibility of Jhumpa Lahiri, who was born in London of Bengali parents and who grew up in Rhode Island, USA, where she is now living. In a way, she is a diasporic author whose sensibility incorporates three worlds—India, the land of her ancestors, England, the land that gave shelter to her parents, and America, the land of her present residence. These three worlds can easily be grouped into two worlds of the East and the West. And Jhumpa Lahiri's sensibility, as witnessed in *Interpreter of Maladies,* forcefully expresses itself in what Meena Alexander calls "a shifting frame of reference, of multiple worlds" (Alexander, 1997, 3). This kind of expatriate or diasporic sensibility is largely concerned with "not only...a basic geographical distinction but also a whole sense of 'interests'" (Said, 1978, 12). The nine short stories contained in *Interpreter of Maladies* powerfully reflect its author's 'shifting frame of reference' and 'whole sense of interests', spanning two worlds of the East and the West and weaving a delightful texture of fictional art.

WORKS CITED

Alexander, Meena (21st Dec., 1997). "Freedom and the Indian Diaspora: An Interview." *The Hindu Literary Review*.

Lahiri, Jhumpa (1999). *Interpreter of Maladies*. New Delhi: Harper Collins Publishers India Ltd.

Said, Edward (1978). *Orientalism*. London: Routledge.

Diasporic Concerns in Jhumpa Lahiri's *Interpreter of Maladies*

10

Abha Shukla Kaushik

The use of the term *diaspora* is quite widespread in discourse of various kinds. It is used to describe the dispersion of a people from their original homeland. For Ashcroft, Griffiths, and Tiffin diaspora cannot be separated from colonialism, as it was this historical condition that led to the displacement of people across the world under different circumstances or forms of compulsion. Ashcroft et al. resist the temptation of dividing the subjects of diaspora into two categories: the people from metropolitan centres who relocated to the colonial peripheries or the colonized who were forced back into centres through processes like slavery. In effect the link between diaspora and colonialism is noted to be by far more complex. Whether or not the people of the diaspora were settlers, migrants, transported convicts, slaves, or labourers is beside the point; what is more apparent is the capacity of colonialism to produce so many varied forms of power that compel people to move. Consequently, the culture produced by diaspora cannot but contain so many resonances of the movement, the imagination of their homelands, sense of tradition, the circumstances of their removal, and the reaction to the places they currently live in. Salman Rushdie has put the dilemma of diaspora in *Imaginary Homelands* that the position of the exile or immigrant is one of the 'profound uncertainties'.

In her essay *Reading Diaspora* Nalini Natarajan argues that "the phenomenon of diasporic populations is by no means new, but its scale in the twentieth century is dramatic" (xiii). Sudesh Mishra, the author of the essay *From Sugar to Masala: Writing by the Indian Diaspora* distinguishes between the old (sugar) and new (masala) diasporic movements. He claims that while the old diasporic writers tend to concentrate on the inner experiences, the new diasporic writers focus on the "threshold zone of intercutting subjectivities that define the experience of migrancy" (287). Diasporic writers continue to be hung up on their national identities even if they may not sometimes be aware of or admit it themselves. The prominent feature of diasporic literature lies in its continued projection of the writer's motherland and its culture. Most Indian diasporic writers set their works in India and not in the adopted land and for this speciality the West finds colourful cultural ethnic shades in diasporic writings. Jhumpa Lahiri, the acclaimed Pulitzer Prize winning writer of *Interpreter of Maladies* can be placed amongst the many writers of new or 'masala' diasporas. Although not all of the stories in *Interpreter of Maladies* are set in America, but all of them deal with characters in diaspora of one sort or another. Very few essential characters in the book live in their original homeland, and, if they do, they represent the first generation in their family, born into a Western culture. Thus, most of the characters in *Interpreter of Maladies* must cope with living in the diaspora in some sense.

In the title story 'Interpreter of Maladies', Das family is on a visit to India, Mr. Kapasi is leading this Indian American family around India. Mr. and Mrs. Das enjoy all things which are Indian. Lahiri depicts the effects of Western colonialism on Indians and Indians in diaspora. The Das family, settled abroad, is afflicted with a sense of exile. Alienation seems to have become their lot. The absence of the sense of belonging that they experience is reflected in the presence of a lingering awareness on their part to clutch at a world that does not belong to them. As a result, the couple is as if drinking its fill of Indian experience. For them the Sun temple at Konark is 'must see', they also enjoy 'jhalmuri'. Mrs. Das is quite a foreigner in her dress—enough to intrigue Mr. Kapasi, their guide who wonders "the family looked Indian but dressed as foreigners did" (43-44). She even carries her own water bottle lest she should catch some infection due to consumption of contaminated water. But she cannot resist enjoying the 'jhalmuri'. The family also enjoys a hearty breakfast at a roadside restaurant. On the one hand, they sip preserved and bottled mango juices with sandwiches, while on the other hand, they also enjoy the typically Indian 'pakoras' for which Lahiri uses a detailed definition as 'onions and potatoes deep fried in grahamflour batter" (54). The attitude of the Das family, all born in America, towards India reveals the fact that they fetishize and imagine an India which is very different from reality although technically it is their homeland. The visitors find that the Chandrabhaga river has dried up, and they can no longer enter the Temple of the Sun "for it had filled with rubble long ago" (57). These images represent the collapse, deterioration, or passing of once important cultural or spiritual values. The story also touches on the themes of love, duty and disillusionment. But the crux of the story lies in the word play—the word *interpreter* acquires several meanings. At one level it is Mr. Kapasi, the guide who works as an interpreter for doctor. Mrs. Das, desperate for advice, confides in him about her extramarital relationship, in the hope that as an 'interpreter of maladies' he would be able to offer an explanation for her unhappiness. Mr. Kapasi himself, unaccustomed to such a request, is at a loss as to how he should interpret her secret. He had been attracted by Mrs. Das's glamour but is later appalled by her cruelty and is unable to interpret his own behaviour and reactions in proper perspective. Finally, in order to get to the heart of the matter he decides to ask her if it is pain or guilt that she feels, and the truth is unfolded. On another level it is the Dases who try to interpret their imaginary 'homeland' with the help from books and guides. Above all, it is the writer who is interpreting various maladies of belonging, of lack of communication, of identity. The story beautifully expresses the dilemma, the difficulty and often the impossibility of communicating emotional pain and affliction to others as well as to one's ownself.

For immigrants, the challenges of exile, the loneliness, the constant sense of alienation, the knowledge of and longing for a lost world, are more explicit and distressing. The question of identity is always a difficult one, but especially so for those who are culturally displaced, as immigrants are. The story entitled

"Mrs. Sen's" in this collection is about a woman who moves with her husband out of India to the United States. She takes charge of taking care of an eleven-year-old American boy. Mrs. Sen tries very hard to become accustomed to the ways and customs of this new country but she is unable to escape from the fact that, "Every thing is there" (113). Everything that Mrs. Sen has known and loved has been left behind in India and the effects of her displacement can be seen in her actions. The story is written from the perspective of a child, who watches his baby sitter, Mrs. Sen, go about her chores, from chopping vegetables with a blade "curved like the prow of a Viking ship" (114) to applying a streak of crushed vermilion to the parting in her hair with the head of a thumbtack, all the time describing the life she reluctantly left behind in Calcutta. The story traces the efforts of a young woman trying to adapt to the lonely life of a docile housewife married to a mathematics professor in an American University. Her life is infested with cultural alienation as she is bored to death as her husband is busy with his job and more so because she misses her Calcutta family, her neighborhood and above all the community feeling that is totally absent in the American culture. Mrs. Sen is a typical Bengali woman for whom fish is the ultimate food. Fish which is an important part of Bengali cuisine becomes an obsession with Mrs. Sen as it is not always that one gets good whole fish in America. The arrival of fish at the local store excites her as much as news from home—from India, and she is always too eager to hold it, to cook it and to serve it to Mr. Sen. Whenever fresh fish arrives in the market, she either entrusts Mr. Sen with the job of bringing it home or else she takes a bus to fetch the fish but is deterred from doing so as other passengers object to the smell. She is still learning to drive, yet when the fish arrives in market the next time she takes a bold step and decides to drive to the store but meets with an accident. Fish becomes the leitmotif in the story. Mrs. Sen's existence as also her survival in an alien land revolves around and depends upon this food item. When she gets it she is happy, and when she is unable to get it for a long time she sulks like a child. For her fish is not only a source of pleasure but it also represents her home, her state, her neighborhood, her family and a friend as it gives her a sense of proximity to her people. Thus fish not only serves as a metaphor but acquires a character as well in the story. It is the only recognizable signpost left in her life—a reassuring bit of the homeland that she clings to in absence of anything else that is meaningful in her life. She wears exquisite saris brought carefully from India but which no longer have any remaining purpose in America. The trips to fish market and the letters from India are the only things which keep her feeling whole while ironically also illuminating her emptiness within. The story addresses the many isolated immigrant women, not just of Indian descent, but of universal origin, through its poignant depiction of woman trying to assimilate but unwilling to let go of the aspects of her life in India that do not fit. Lahiri presents evidence for the feelings of disorientation associated with immigration through subtle details that emphasize the cross-cultural differences that are the feeling factors in plot development. Like Mrs. Sen, most of Lahiri's characters move between the Indian subcontinent and the United States. They date, emigrate and work across cultural and national borders. Her stories are rendered more powerful by the sense of cultural transition and loss. "Everything is there", Mrs. Sen says of India, but the fact remains that she herself no longer is. Lahiri's Indian Americans struggle for dignity—they are people stranded in a country and a culture that is not their own but which demands conformity from them.

Navigating between the Indian traditions they've inherited and the baffling new world they are living in, the characters in Lahiri's stories seek love beyond the barriers of culture and generations. "When Mr. Pirzada came to Dine" is a powerful story, set in New England in 1971, exploring the subject of partition—the division of India and Pakistan by the British in 1947 and afterwards the partition of Pakistan and Bangladesh in 1971. The story describes the growing awareness of a ten-year-old girl growing up in a Boston suburb of her Indianness, when her parents befriend a visiting Bangladeshi botanist, whose stay in the US coincides with the Bangladeshi war of independence in 1971. Separated from his wife and seven daughters, whose fates are uncertain, he takes his meals with the only Indian family in their small college town. The ten-year-old Lilia observes similarities between her Bengali parents and Mr. Pirzada, a Pakistani from Dacca. They "spoke the same language, laughed at the same jokes, looked more or less the same...ate pickled mangoes with their meals, ate rice every night for supper with their hands" (25). This fact of similarity is understood by a small girl. In a foreign land the fact of belonging to a different country becomes meaningless as though their countries are different, yet their cultures are the same. The young girl who feels totally at ease in the presence of Mr. Pirzada, who is also a 'foreigner' in a sense to her, can't believe that her American school teaches nothing about the Pakistani civil war that preoccupies her parents and the gentleman who joins them every night for dinner. She observes Mr. Pirzada as he scrutinizes war footage from home and the network news even if it is only aired as a passing reference, "As he watched, he had an immovable expression on his face, composed but alert, as if someone were giving him directions to an unknown destination" (31). The scenes revolving around the preparation of dinner, which was to be eaten while watching the evening news, with mother at the stove, father snacking on the cashews as he leans against the fridge and the young girl interacting with them—both are evocative of Indian American life in a way that can only be described by someone who has lived such a life. The story not only depicts the oneness of people belonging to geographically two different countries but also comments on the subtle, though ultimately noticeable effects of Western colonialism on Indians and Indians in Diaspora. Lilia notes that "we learned American history, of course, and American geography. That year, and every year it seemed we began by studying the Revolutionary War" (27). And when she tries to read about India in her school library, her teacher Miss Kenyon discourages her saying there was no reason to consult books on India as it was not a part of her field of study. It is evident that Lilia's parents, because of socio-economical reasons and perhaps due to cultural inferiority, do partially assimilate to the American way of life, but at the same time they also make a conscious effort to cling to their roots in India and such a paradox makes it more difficult for the young girl to decipher which place she belongs to. On the one hand, she leads a very Westernized life. She goes to an American school; associates with American children; celebrates their festivals like the Halloween; her father works with the Americans; her neighbours are American; she speaks English; she watches American television and she is fully exposed to the American way of life. On the other hand, she is exposed to a very Indian way of life, albeit only in the confines of her own home where her mother cooks Indian food, her parents speak Bengali; and they are forever concerned about India and what is happening there. The story underlines the fact that diasporic literature focuses on cultural states and is not bothered about the geographic borders of the nation states. Thus, Lilia is made aware of the differences between living in suburban America and life in less stable parts of the world, i.e. the South Asian subcontinent. A concrete difference in diasporic experiences is discernible in Lilia's relationship to America in contrast with her parents' relationship to America. Her parents' roots will forever be in India. For them India is an actual and concrete place that will be 'home' in their hearts forever. They are tied to the memories of India they carry with them and they are constantly struggling to adjust to a new country and a new way of life. Their daughter's diasporic experience is considerably different—she is not tied to a specific place. India to her is the "imaginary homeland", not home, neither is America. But then to be 'unhomed is not to be homeless' as Homi Bhabha has pointed out in 'The Location of Culture'. It is the gray area between America and India, the two places, lifestyles and cultures that she has to finally recognize as her home.

Another story of Lahiri's collection of nine, 'The Third and Final Continent', addresses the realities of arranged marriages and the long process of assimilation into American culture from an Indian perspective. Perhaps modeled upon aspects of her parents' lives in the United States, Lahiri presents a first person account of an Indian man arranging for the arrival of his new bride as he lives under the roof of an aged American landlady. The vivid differences between his bachelor life in a room in this woman's house and the journey that he takes while learning who his bride is boldly comments on the cultural differences and similarities in the two cultures. Senses of isolation and a coming together in order to survive are evident in both of these relationships. At the end of the story, Lahiri introduces the idea of loss of cultural identification through passing generations by mentioning the college going child of the couple. They bring him home to 'eat rice with his hands and speak Bengali' which are 'things [they] sometimes worry he will no longer do after [they] die' (197). Lahiri presents a couple whose only remaining connection with the country of their origin has a definitive death with their own end because the assimilation of their son into American culture leaves no room for their own cultural orientation.

The stories in the collection *Interpreter of Maladies* are a testament to Lahiri's versatility as a writer. She has the ability to change cultural perspective as easily as a bilingual person's ability to shift from language to language. She does not paint pretty pictures. Her canvas is made up of details that make up the reality of everyday life. Most of the stories are written from a perspective that is between cultures. The characters are not traumatized refugees but are negotiating a path in a country (America) that seems to provide opportunities (as in "A Temporary Matter," "The Third and Final Continent," "Mrs. Sen's," "When Mr. Pirzada Came to Dine"); or they are the Americanized children of such Indian families (as in "Interpreter of Maladies", "This Blessed House"). Ties to the Asian sub-continent may be strong or weak, primary text or subtext, but they are ever-present. Living between cultures lends an extra layer of complexity to situations and relationships that are difficult in and of themselves.

WORKS CITED

Ashcroft, Bill, Gareth Griffiths and Helen Tiffin. *Key Concepts in Post-Colonial Studies.* London and New York: Routledge, 1998.

Bhabha, Homi. *The Location of Culture.* London and New York: Routledge, 1994.

Lahiri, Jhumpa. *Interpreter of Maladies.* New York: Houghton Mifflin Company, 1999.

Natarajan, Nalini. "Reading Diaspora." *Writers of Indian Diaspora*. Ed. Emmanuel S. Nelson. Connecticut: Greenwich Press, 1993.

Rushdie, Salman. *Imaginary Homelands*. London: Granta Books, 1992.

Sudesh, Mishra. "From Sugar to Masala: Writing by the Indian Diaspora." *A History of Indian Literature in English*. Ed. Arvind Krishna Melhotra. New York: Columbia University Press, 2003.

Tales from Firozsha Baag: Prologue to Rohinton Mistry's Fiction

11

J.P. Savita

Rohinton Mistry's literary odyssey started in 1983 with the publication of a short story entitled "One Sunday". His first book *Tales from Firozsha Baag* (1987) was an instant success and was short-listed for the Governor General's Award. It contain eleven short stories dealing with the haps and mishaps in the lives of the residents of Firozsha Baag, a ghetto-like colony of Parsis in postcolonial Bombay (India). That obviously makes this book much more than a collection of stray short stories. It is a germinal book, a virtual gateway to the other more ambitious works of Rohinton Mistry. It successfully sets the tone and tenor of his subsequent novels.

When *Tales from Firozsha Baag* appeared on the literary scene, its author had lived in Canada for well over a decade. He had migrated to Toronto at the age of twenty-three. His birth and upbringing in Bombay make him an eminently suitable writer for witnessing the last bright sparks of the existence of the Parsis in India. This is the most significant point to remember about Mistry. He is a Parsi Zoroastrian born and brought up in Bombay (now Mumbai). Demographically, the Parsis are a minuscule minority in the world—just about one lakh, seventy per cent living in some small pockets of the metropolitan city of Bombay. During pre-colonial times the Parsis of India maintained a low profile and jealously guarded their ethnic identity. During the colonial period they enjoyed a privileged status as brokers between the British and other Indians. They became very Westernized and identified almost completely with the colonial masters. This in turn was bound to create as it did create problems in postcolonial India where their social and economic status was much downgraded. The Parsi colonies were no more their exclusive Goshen but decaying fortresses where they were (and still are) living with what Bharucha rightly calls "a siege mentality" (25). Some, of course, were prompted to move to the West and shed their Indian identities. This too has resulted in psychological trauma, as in the West they have been lumped together with Asian groups—specifically Indian. This is broadly the thematic plank of the *Tales from Firozsha Baag*, indeed of the entire corpus of Mistry's fiction published hitherto.

Unlike most diasporic writers who indulge in the luxury of writing about what Salman Rushdie terms 'Imaginary homelands', Mistry is emphatically a 'Bombay writer'—an insider who has observed nay lived the milieu of his fiction. Even where the foreign factor intrudes as in the concluding story of *Tales from Firozsha Baag*, the chief protagonist is a Bombayite Parsi whose Parsiness (or parsipanno) receives a severe beating in Canada. Indeed he is more or less Mistry's own alter ego in the story. The distance in terms of time and place has enabled the author to transcend sentimentalism. If it is nostalgia, it is nostalgia conjured as re-memory. In an interview Mistry termed his creative process as "imagination ground through the mill of memory". It is, he further adds "impossible to separate the too ingredients" (Interview. Lambert). And what an esemplastic imagination it is which according to Coleridge "dissolves, diffuses, dissipates in order to recreate". To quote S. Ramaswamy, "Remembering, re-enacting, recreating that place, time, people with accuracy, understanding and insight is the vision of Rohinton Mistry" (54).

Tales from Firozsha Baag is not just a bunch of diverse short stories. It is to be treated as a complete whole—a one-unit kaleidoscopic picture of the Parsi community in post-Independence Bombay. The reader here feels like a curious visitor to this Parsi colony, consisting of old dilapidated quarters with leaking roof and peeling paint. He is an honoured guest in every household, each one with one or more odd characters. They are Parsis and somewhat wary of outsiders. Even so, skeletons in some of the cupboards are laid open. The residents have so much in common—their rituals and customs, then own brands of costumes and cuisine, even their special lingo, their scatological humour, peculiar nicknames, their feuds and squabbles, then prejudices and predilections. For all these superficial peculiarities they are basically the stuff which humanity is made of. So much happens—so much of comedy, even farce and horseplay; so much of tragedy—death, murder, helpless aged couples whose children have emigrated to US or Canada. So on and so forth. On the whole, a very illuminating if somewhat touching picture.

The eleven tales of this collection are like eleven chapters of a giant novel. In its own right it can be called an 'episodic' novel. So is *Pickwick Papers*. Only *Pickwick Papers* is 'person oriented' whereas *Tales from Firozsha Baag* is 'locale oriented'. It is like Malgudi and R. Mistry is, as it were, R.K. Narayan in the making one may as well call it *Sthala Purana* the name given by Raja Rao to his magnum opus. Incidentally, the narrative technique adopted in *Kanthapura* is not much different from the one used by that resident story teller of Firozsha Baag, Nariman Hansotia in 'Squatter'. The carry-on of names from one tale to another further provides a commonality between them—Rustomji, the curmudgeon, the ubiquitous Najamai of the refrigerator fame, the homoerotic Jahangir Bulsara, the Boyce boys Percy and Kesri continue to appear, disappear and reappear.

Above all is the ethnic detailing—the typical and authentic ambience, Parsi ambience. The very first story *Auspicious Occasion* is symptomatic. *Auspicious Occasion* is *Behram roji,* the main Parsi festival. Rustomji in the beginning is as snobbish and haughty as a Parsi can possibly be. His wife Mehroo (twenty years younger to him) is pious and given to much praying and *agiary* going. India is firmly kept out of their Parsi home and the only contact they have with the non-Parsis is through their servants, mostly a cleaning woman always called *Ganga* by Parsis. As Rustomji steps out in his sparkling white *dugli* (coat) and carefully brushed *Pheytoe* (head gear) a *ghaati* (a pejorative term used by Parsis for low class natives) lets loose a *paan* spittle on Rustomji's *dugli*. Instead of being intimidated by his ravings and rantings, the *ghaatis* get together and almost beat him up. He escapes only by playing the clown—dislodging his dentures and spitting them out on his palms. The incident is symbolic of the downgrading of Parsi image in decolonised India. Old habits die hard. In *The Ghost of Firozha Baag* (the only story with a non-Parsi narrator) the Catholic ayah from Goa—Jacqueline (whose name is consistently mispronounced by her Parsi employers as Jaakaylee) complains that the Parsi "thought they were like British only ruling India side by side" (46). The Parsi nostalgia for the Raj can be seen in *White Hairs and Cricket.* The three stories—*Squatter, Lend Me Your Light* and *Swimming Lessons* highlight the pathos and loneliness of ageing Parsis whose children are in a Western diaspora. There the children's dreams of being an elite community end, more often than not, in nightmares. The 'we-consciousness' is nowhere more conspicuous than in the story entitled *Paying Guests.* Here the landlady (Khorshedbai), fighting a case for eviction against her tenants (Boman and Kashmira), would not stoop to ask a Muslim neighbor to testify against a fellow Parsi.

The whole text of the *Tales of Ferozsha Baag* is studded with Parsiana-Zoroastrian festivals, and rituals—*Behram roje, navroje,* Parsi temple, the tower of silence, the Parsi calendar; Parsi customs—*charam* (fourth day ceremony), *dushmoo* (tenth day ceremony), *musra* (first month ceremony), Parsi costumes—*dugli* (coat), *pheytoe* (head gear), *kutsis* (the sacred thread worn by Parsi)—*mathbanoo* (head scarf worn by Parsi ladies), Parsi cuisine—*dhansak masala, sali boti* etc. etc. In *Exercisers* when Jahangir's parents discover that he is in love with 'an unsuitable girl', they take him (in vain of course) to Bhagwan Baba, a Hindoo Godman in the hope that he would do the miracle of dissuading him. Here is an example of Parsis coming out of their hard-shell and seeking nearness to the Hindoos.

Despite this thick ethnic coloring and despite his touching (in later work vehemently projecting) socio-political issues, R. Mistry has repeatedly denied that he has any agenda *per se*. He considers himself first and foremost a story-teller whose chief aim is 'to tell a darn good story' (Interview. Gibson). No doubt he has triumphantly succeeded in this prime aim of fiction writing. In this he betrays a strange family-likeness to the Victorians, those masters of story-telling. Characters like Najamai, Nariman, Hinsotia and Sarosh/Sid irresistibly remind one of the characters of Dickens—that master character monger and entertainer. Yet there the comparison should stop. Dickens' is the art of a cartoonist. He exaggerates as much in his characterization as in his use of humor and pathos. Mistry's world, on the contrary, is perfectly life size. In fact realism is his forte. Far from a cartoonist, he gives the impression of a professional paparazzo, out to take shots of Firozsha housing complex and its residents as they are—warts and all.

Humour is all pervading (along with a deep under current of compassion). Sometimes, it is bordering on the farcical (as in *Squatter*). Often, it is apiece with the overall complexion of the place and the persons living there. After all Firozsha Baag is a ghetto like place, a virtual Harlem in the heart of Bombay. Most of the residents are lower middle class Parsis, bereft of modern amenities. There is just one refrigerator in the whole complex. Only two persons own cars of very old models. There is no park. The usual pastime of street urchins is stoning cats or killing rats with out-of-use tennis racquets. They gleefully mouth obscenities such as even Krishna Sobti would hesitate to put into print. There are unabashed if amusing allusions to female anatomy, masturbation and even sodomy. One typical example of scatological humour is the story *Squatters* in which Sarosh or Sid the protagonist is a Canadian immigrant. He has to face a plethora of problems because of his squatting habit. Thanks to his recalcitrant bowels, the land of milk and honey is for him just a pain in the posterior. Pesi, the scapegrace only son of Dr. Burjor Modi, is a ferting virtuouso who can break wind at will and modulate it in diverse tones. He is nicknamed *Pesi Paadmarroo* and he wears this sobriquet with considerable pride. All this, if taken out of context, may offend a sophisticated taste. Otherwise it is quite in keeping with the over-all milieu of Firozsha Baag. One is reminded of Chaucer's quoting of Plato—in defense of his use of broad language in the *Canterbury Tales*—"Words must be cousin to the deeds"—a standard which Mistry triumphantly maintains in all his works of which *Tales from Firozsha Baag* is justifiably the prologue.

And this Prologue has an epilogue too, the last story entitled *Swimming Lessons* merits a special mention. It is the only story set in Canada though even here the chief protagonist Kesri is a Bombayite Parsi youth. More importantly this story serves as a sort of self-reflexive post-script to this collection—a self-critique. The reflexive element, printed in italics, is routed through the reactions of Kesri's parents to his stories. The diasporic writer's need to write about the homeland left behind is dealt with in the father's evaluation of his son's work. Was it to pre-empt Parsi annoyance at far from flattering portrayal? Or was Mistry's trying to work out a theory of his brand of fiction as well as the creative process that went into its making? Arriving at answers to these questions requires further in-depth analysis.

WORKS CITED

Bharucha, Nilufer E. "When Old Tracks are Lost: Rohinton Mistry's Fiction as Diasporic Discourse." *Fiction of Rohinton Mistry: Critical Studies*. Ed. Jaydipsingh Dodia. New Delhi: Prestige Books, 1998.

Gibson, Stacey. Interview of Rohinton Mistry.

Lambert, Angela. "Touched with Fire." Interview. *The Guardian*, April 26, 2002.

Ramaswamy, S. "Local Colour in the *Tales from Firozsha Baag.*" *Fiction of Rohinton Mistry: Critical Studies*. Ed. Jaydipsingh Dodia. New Delhi: Prestige Books, 1998.

Rohinton Mistry's *Family Matters:* A Diasporic and Ethnic Text

12

Malti Agarwal

The literary odyssey of Rohinton Mistry which started in 1983 with the publication of his first story "One Sunday" passed through his collection of short stories *Tales from Firozsha Baag,* published by Penguin Canada in 1987 and was followed by his first novel *Such a Long Journey.* This first novel brought Mistry unprecedented success as he won the Governor General's Award for fiction. The second work of Mistry which appeared in 1991 was laid in the backdrop of the war, fought between India and Pakistan in 1971. The second novel of Mistry *A Fine Balance,* published in 1996, takes into account the detailed descriptions of emergency imposed by Mrs. Indira Gandhi in 1975 which eroded the fundamental rights granted to the Indian citizens by the Constitution of India. His latest novel *Family Matters* which came out in 2002 took Mistry back to Bombay and the Parsi people. Rohinton Mistry's texts seem to be preoccupied with the homeland and the political and the social environment of the place of his birth. His books as the diasporic writings are concerned with some basic representation such as "how the self is represented, seen and remembered against the backdrop of the past" (Jain 9). Mistry has been living in Toronto (Canada) from 1975 yet he has deep-rooted love for his native place India. Consequently, all his novels and short stories focus on the life lived by the Bombayites and especially the Parsis. They all reflect the novelist's continuing attachment to his birth-place though he stays thousands of kilometres away from his old home. The works of the diasporic writers such as of Rohinton Mistry are characterized by the salient features of the diasporic literature. They display the personal and psychic trauma, a sense of loss and nostalgia, despair, dislocation, exile, alienation and memory of the past. Emmanuel Nelson has rightly observed that the "haunting presence of India" lies at the core of diasporic fiction by writers of Indian descent, together with the "anguish of personal loss" that an awareness of India engenders (xv).

Family Matters, till date the finest novel of Mistry, is centred round the aged Parsi, retired Professor of English. The details of the life of Nariman Vakeel provide the novelist an opportunity to open up the whole vistas of human emotions such as love, hate and guilt. This seventy nine-year-old Professor lives with his two grown-up step children—Coomy and Jal. These three though make a heterogeneous group yet on compulsion live together, sharing the chill and the sunshine of human relationships. Coomy who does not like her step father is anxious about his safety. "You'll drive me crazy", said Coomy, "My heart is going dhuk-dhuk, wondering if you collapsed or something" (4). The interest of the book, to a great extent, lies in its being a book of compassion, a book dealing with the warmth of human bonds and native customs. Mistry, an Indian who now lives in Canada and writes from Canada, is a writer of Indian Diaspora who like most diasporic writers writes about the contemporary conditions, prevailing in the homeland. Jopi Nyman rightly quotes the words of Susheila Nasta as put by her in her recent book *Home Truths: Fictions of the South Asian Diaspora in Britain (2002):* "for diaspora, does not only create an unrequited desire for a lost homeland but also a homing desire, a desire to reinvent and rewrite home as much as a desire to come to terms with an exile from it. Diaspora is, therefore, as much settlement as displacement" (Qtd. Nyman Preface). The diasporic writers in their search of a hybrid space keep their traditions, native customs and religions alive and also try to assimilate the culture of the alien land. Jopi Nyman in Preface to *The Atlantic Literary Review's* special issue on *Diasporic Indian Fiction* refers to this special feature of the diasporic fiction: "As a result, fictions of diaspora are not necessarily nostalgic lamentations but texts actively redefining the migrants' sense of self and home, often showing their subjects re-entering spaces and sites once important to their families" (Preface VI). Rohinton Mistry, writing from Canada, recalls the Parsi customs and the ills which beset Bombay in the mid-1990s. But the focus in the present novel is mainly on the portrayal of the human bonds which characterize the Indian character. To quote Bharucha, "It is a book which is very 'big' in compassion—it is indeed Mistry's most compassionate book to date. At the age of 50, from his Canadian point of vantage, Mistry has viewed the life of a middle-class Parsi family in Bombay in the mid-1990s" (168).

The Septuagenarian protagonist, a patient of Parkinson's disease is looked after by his step-children as the unmarried adults in India stay with their parents. Coomy, despite her hatred for her step-father, ties the laces of his shoes and is worried to notice the tremors in the hands of Vakeel. But she is resentful of the nuptial bliss, being enjoyed by her half-sister Roxana, born of her mother and step-father. The love of Jal and Coomy for their half-sister was complete and full when they were at fourteen and twelve because then "they were not prey to the complicated feelings of jealousy, neglect, rivalry, or even hatred, which newborns evoke in siblings closer in age" (9). But the childhood bonds which were not tainted by 'half' or 'step' title become weak when Nariman falls down and breaks his ankle. Jal's excitement at having the baby in his arms, her clutching at his finger now disappears and Coomy's delight at holding little Roxana also suddenly evaporates as once she exclaimed in delight, "Look, she's blowing bubbles, just like my ring!" (11).

Family Matters has several flash-backs when Nariman remembers his past days. Nariman when a young boy loved a Catholic girl Lucy Braganza. But he has to break his liaison with Lucy as the Parsis cannot marry their offsprings outside their community nor the Catholic parents of Lucy allow her to enter into inter-religious marriage. Under the law of bigotry, such inter-religions or inter-communal marriages were forbidden. And eventually a man forty-year old who failed to 'preserve that balance between tradition and modernness' (15) and who was found "incapable of falling in love with a Parsi girl" (14) was married to a Parsi widow Yasmin Contractor, the mother of two children—Jal and Coomy. Mistry, thus, brings into light the Parsi orthodoxy which at times ruins the life of the promising youths.

Nariman's agonies whether he is staying with the Contractors or with the Chenoys form the axis on which the main plot revolves. Coomy and Jal decide to transfer their step-father to the Pleasant Villa to stay with Roxana, biologically their step-sister. Poor helpless Nariman has nothing to say except that "Lying in bed, here or there, is all the same to me. But it will be difficult for them, in such a small flat" (75). The old man's stay at this two-room flat of Roxana leads to many hot exchanges between wife and husband. The two loving grandchildren of Nariman take great pains to dissolve or diffuse the rising tensions in the house. Ultimately, the Chenoy family overcomes all ordeals since their love for each other cements their relationship and they learn the lesson of self-sacrifice. Yezad, Jahangir and Murad—all the three do their best to tackle in their own way the deficiency of money. Yezad plays Matka, Jahangir takes bribe from his classmate when he was the class monitor and Murad walks home to save bus fare.

Nature, eventually, settles the score. Coomy has made Jal to create holes and cracks in the ceiling of the room. The post collapses which results in the death of Edul and Coomy. The *Pleasant Villa* is sold and the entire family shifts to the *Chateau Felicity* to live forever happily. The book has an epilogue which establishes the fact that history repeats itself. Murad, the elder son of Yezad, falls in love with a non-Parsi girl which leads to friction in the family. It seems to echo the love story of Nariman and Lucy, the non-Parsi girl.

Rohinton Mistry, a Parsi Zoroastrian, was in diaspora even in India. Bharucha, while analyzing this dimension of Rohinton Mistry's life, writes, "However, Mistry is also a Parsi Zoroastrian and a person whose ancestors were forced into exile by the Islamic conquest of Iran, he was in diaspora even in India. This informs his writings with the experience of multiple displacements" (24). In order to save their ethnic identity, the Parsis observe all religious rites and rituals. As Parsis are in an ethnic minority so the religious identity is of paramount importance to them. Bharucha while talking about the identities puts the assertions of ethnicity within the ambit of the first/primary circle. He adds, "For Parsis in the Indian diaspora, the fact of being a Parsi Zoroastrian is racial and religious identity; then comes the Nationalist identity; then the wider transnational identity" (58-59). In *Family Matters,* Mistry discusses at length the Parsi religion, customs and rituals. On Nariman Vakeel's birthday, the Chenoys and the Contractors assemble at *Chateau Felicity*. Mistry describes some of the rituals, regularly observed by the Parsis. Coomy enters with the silver thurible, ready for loban. Her head is now covered with a white mulmul scarf. Here is an excerpt from the text to throw light on other customs, observed by the Parsis:

"The fragrance of frankincense delighted Roxana, for ritual and religion meant more to her than it ever had to Yezad. After her mother's sudden death, her training had been taken over by the Contractor side of the family, and Nariman's heavy conscience had refused them nothing. They had taught for the prayers, performed her navjote, taken her to the fire-temple for every holy day" (23). The silver thurible, a holy object, filled Roxana with reverence and then it is offered to each person for obeisance. To Roxana, loban smoke was like "angels and fareshtas floating through the house" (23). The novel relates a complete transformation of Yezad who observes all religious rituals. He now goes to the fire-temple everyday, offers prayers and finds solace in the contact of God. To him, the fire-temple is now "a real oasis in the midst of this big, mad city" (268).

There are references to navjote ceremony also. Besides, the Parsis are conscious of their racial identity. In the present novel, Dr. Fitter regrets the deterioration of the race. He comments, "when you think of our forefathers, the industrialists and shipbuilders who established the foundation of modern India, the philanthropists who gave us our hospitals and schools and libraries and baags, what lustre they brought to our community and the nation. And this incompetent fellow cannot look after his father" (45).

Parsis are known for certain specific things, *Family Matters* illustrates the 'Parsi knack of being ethnically conscious' as Mr. Kapur, the proprietor of *Bombay Sporting,* praises the Parsis' and especially Yezad's honesty, "oh, don't be modest, the Parsi reputation for honesty is well-known. And even if it's a myth—there is no myth without truth, no smoke without fire" (134). Parsis' beliefs and their aversions have also been mentioned by the novelist. Nariman tells his grandson, Jehangoo, of Parsis' aversion for cats and their belief in spiders and cocks. He says: "No, No cats. Parsi families never keep cats. They consider them bad luck, because cats hate water, they never take a bath" (139). He tells how Parsis don't kill spiders, and they only eat the female chicken, never a cock—"You must know that, from the story of Zuhaak the Evil one" (139). Mistry's texts preserve a record of how the Parsis lived and preserved their ethno-religious identity. As the Parsis are allergic to conversion into Parsi religion and also are averse to inter-religious marriages, Nariman and later Murad are not allowed to marry the non-Parsi girl. Mistry's texts are often termed as "Nostalgia Writing". The diasporic writers often have the pangs of nostalgia when they see their past as present and create an imaginary homeland. Though Mistry does not approve the nostalgic writings yet he himself admits in an interview with Lakhani that "I think in Bombay and India, my imagination is engaged by that place still after these years...".

Whether it is *Such a Long Journey* or *A Fine Balance* or *Family Matters,* Mistry uses memory and remembering as a narrative technique. Bharucha rightly termed it as 'nostalgia conjured as re-memory', the term that he used in relation to *Tales from Ferozsha Baag.* In this connection, he in his book *Rohinton Mistry: Ethnic Enclosures and Transcultural Spaces* quotes the words of Edward Said, "exile is punishing but also rewarding. Once you have lost your homeland, it cannot be recovered as paradise" [Interview with Padgaonkar]. Uma Parameswaran in her write up *Dispelling the Spells of Memory: Another Approach to Reading Our Yesterdays* refers to this dynamics of the diasporic literature, she writes, "Indian diasporic literature, then, differs from other North American diasporas in its retrieval and recording of Exile. Wilson Harris says that if one lives in a country without history, one has to discover it or invent it, for Memory is the cornerstone of identity". These diasporic writers—the exiles, emigrants or expatriates—look back perhaps because they "hesitate to write about their new homeland, as if they did, they would write as outsiders—persons who did not belong" (Bharucha 67). But Mistry has no anguish of exile. He quite sensitively records the past—'a past that has changed in his absence'.

Mistry's text *Family Matters* illustrates his use of remembering the past or more precisely reinventing the past. The novel deals with some parochial as well as national issues. The Babri Mosque riots have been discussed at length. There is a reference to an old Parsi couple that was burned down by the goondas who thought Muslims were hiding in that flat. The involvement of the Shiv-Sena in the Babri Masjid riots has been resented by Mr. Kapur in a harsh tone. Shiv Sena, he says, was involved in looting and burning, police helping rioters, with holding assistance in Muslim localities (133). Husain, a peon in *Bombay Sporting*, is a victim of Babri Mosque riot in which he lost his wife and children. To Mr. Kapur, Bomaby is everything. He feels sorry for the present state of Bombay where "politics is filthy, soiling everything it touches" (135). He yells, "My beloved Bombay is being raped" (135).

Corruption in India has become the order of the day. And, unfortunately, politics is breeding it fast. Mark the conversation going on among Nariman's family members:

"Corruption is in the air we breathe. This nation specializes in turning honest people into crooks. Right, chief?"

"The answer, unfortunately, is yes".

"The country has gone to the dogs. And not well-bred dogs either, but pariahs".

"May be the BJP and Shiv Sena coalition will improve things", said Jal. "We should give them a chance".

Yezad laughed, "If a poisonous snake was in front of you, would you give it a chance? These two parties encouraged the Hindutva extremists to destroy the Babri Mosque" (28-29).

The family criticizes the Shiv Sainiks angrily as they are the false people. Their double standards enrage the family. While, on the one hand, they pose to be the staunch supporters of Indian culture, on the other, they promote the degenerating Western culture by organizing a concert by Michael Jackson. Later in the text, a non-Parsi technician in a hospital, Mr. Rangarajan, who is attending on the Professor, expresses his wish of immigrating from corrupt India to some Western country. He bitterly regrets India's inability to produce one great leader, a Mahatma despite her five-thousand-year-old civilization and nine hundred million people because the Indians need a Mahatma these days. At this, Nariman aptly remarks—"All we get instead are micro-mini atmas" (47). And perhaps these mini atmas wont improve even in a foreign land. The corruption, prevailing in Bombay, is related by Jha differently: "There are quite a few sub-plots revealing the encroachments of a vicious, corrupting world. The troubles in Roxana's house are paralleled in the city of Bombay, ruled by the gangsters like Shiv Sena, "who oppress Muslims as they preserve India from western festivities and morals" (158). Unfortunately, Yezad's boss Mr. Kapur who wants to save his Bombay is killed by the Shiv Sena.

Mistry attacks fiercely at a widespread evil in Mumbai—the Matka. For most of the people Matka was a harmless bit of fun but Yezad once falls a victim to it not for fun but to make both ends meet. Matka was flourishing in Bombay due to the politician-criminal-police nexus. Most shocking is the fact that Matka finances Shiv Sena machinery and thus "in some ways Matka is Bombay and Bombay is Matka" (179).

Further Yezad and Vilas lament over growing violence in Bombay. Vilas finds himself helpless as he does not know how to tell his client that "life is not an Amitabh Bachchan's movie" and also that "justice is a mirage" (181).

Bhaskar, Vilas and Yezad deplore and condemn the prevailing conditions of the nation where under the veil of *Hamara Bharat Mahaan* and much progress in satellite T.V., e-mail, best software designers in the world, the common man is fighting tooth and nail for his happiness and dignity. Rohinton here refers to a novel about the Emergency, the Sanjay sterilization scheme and other horrors related to Emergency. It seems to be an echo of Mistry's own novel, *A Fine Balance* which depicted the days of Emergency in India in 1975. Mark the pungency, latent in Mistry's words:

> A while back, I read a novel about the Emergency. A big book, full of horrors, real as life. But also full of life and the laughter and dignity of ordinary people. One hundred per cent honest—made me laugh and cry as I read it. But some reviewers said no, no, things were not that bad. Especially foreign critics. You know how they come here for two weeks and become experts. One poor woman whose name I can't remember made such a hash of it, she had to be a bit pagal, defending Indira, defending the Sanjay sterilization scheme, defending the entire Emergency—you felt sorry for her even though she was a big professor at some big university in England. What to do? People are afraid to accept the truth. As T.S. Eliot wrote, "Humankind cannot bear very much reality". (181)

Immigration is another vital issue that has been discussed in the text. Yezad (as Mr. Rangarajan also) yearns for migrating to Canada. But soon the dream of immigration shatters into pieces when Yezad comes down to the world of reality. Mistry comments, "The immigration story used to have two parts: dream and reality. But over the years the dream—of prosperity, house, car, C.D. player, computer, clean air, snow, lakes, mountains, ambulance—had been renounced, since it was never going to come true" (215). Mr. M.M. Mazobashi, the Immigration Officer's rudeness and his abusing Yezad and the Indians change his mind. He reacts to his rudeness immediately, "You, sir, are a rude and ignorant man, a disgrace to your office and country. You have sat here abusing us, abusing Indians and India, one of the many countries your government drains of its brainpower, the brainpower that is responsible for your growth and prosperity. Instead of having the grace to thank us, you spew your prejudices and your bigoted ideas. You, whose people suffered racism and xenophobia in Canada, where they were Canadian citizens, put in camps like prisoners of war—you, sir, might be expected, more than anyone else, to understand and embody the more enlightened Canadian ideals of multiculturalism. But if you are anything to go by, then Canada is a gigantic hoax" (219). Here the novelist is critiquing Canada and Canadian multiculturalism. Eventually, Yezad gave up forever the idea of applying again some day for migrating to Canada. He tore into pieces all papers related to migration and makes Nariman speak, "I think emigration is an enormous mistake. The biggest anyone can make in their life. The loss of home leaves a hole that never fills" (220). Nariman here seems to voice the feelings of his creator.

However, Mistry is not averse to Canada or Canadian setting as he in an interview with Dirk Bennett has said that "If a story comes to me with a Canadian setting, I will do it.... I am quite open to it, in fact I would welcome it, it would be a new challenge and that ultimately is what makes me write." Yet Mistry lauds Bombay and has set his books mainly in Bombay. Mr. Kapur in *Family Matters* says, "You know my problem? I am one who loves Bombay not wisely, but too well" (264). In an interview with Indu Sariya, Mistry frankly admits that "Bombay is as viable a city for fiction as is New York or Paris".

By and large, Mistry's texts are not marked by nostalgic lamentations yet like other diasporic writers his texts also have occasional lapses of nostalgia. *Family Matters* also has some nostalgic overtones. Mistry feels nostalgic for the place where he grew up. He remembers his own school teachers—pretty female and fierce male masters when he deals with Jehangir's school—St. Xavier's which was Mistry's own alma matter. In the form of Yezad, he remembers "those happy days, when a week of school was a lifetime, rich and complete; in a week, strangers might become dear friends, battles could be lost and won, whole kingdoms acquired, for time worked differently then" (243). In the form of Yezad's boss, Mr. Kapur, he expresses his concern for renaming of streets and buildings of Bombay. Later he emerges as an idealistic worshipper of Bombay that like Canada's mosaic of cultures assimilates the people of different ethno-religious groups. Mr. Kapur asserts,

"Bombay is like a religion.... Bombay makes room for everybody. Migrants, businessmen, perverts, politicians, holy men, gamblers, beggars, wherever they come from, whatever caste or class, the city welcomes them and turns them into Bombayites" (313-14).

Family Matters, acclaimed as till date the finest novel of Mistry, is read as a Bombay book—"Very much diasporic discourse where from the bird's eye-view provided by the twenty-first century and the wide-angle secured by the location in Canada, Mistry has viewed life in Bombay in the 1990s. However, as he had left for Canada in the 1970s, this is a Bombay which is not so much re-created, as actually 'created', from newspaper reports, visits to the city and visiting friends and relatives from Bombay" (Bharucha 208). Besides, it is read as an ethnocentric text which portrays the Parsi customs and traditions as practised by the Bombayites. In the text, Mistry, thus, deals with multiple issues which rock the life of the Indians. To quote Daruwalla, *Family Matters* "tells the story of familial love and affection, of personal and political corruption, the religious complexity, the power of memory to keep truth alive, and the ultimate peril of memory denied".

WORKS CITED

Bharucha, Nilufer E. *Rohinton Mistry: Ethnic Enclosures and Transcultural Spaces.* Jaipur and New Delhi: Rawat Publications, 2003.

Daruwalla, Keki N. *The Hindustan Times.* New Delhi, Sunday, May 26, 2002.

Jain, Jasbir. Series Editor's Preface. *Rohinton Mistry. Ethnic Enclosures and Transcultural Spaces,* by Nilufer E. Bharucha. Jaipur and New Delhi: Rawat Publications, 2003.

Jha, Parmanand. "Ties and Trials: Rohinton Mistry's *Family Matters." The Indian Journal of English Studies.* Vol. XL, 2002-03.

Mistry, Rohinton. *Family Matters.* United States of America: Vintage International, 2002. (All references of the text are from this edition.)

——. "Interview with Dirk Bennett." www. artsworld.com

——. "Interview with Indu Saraiya." *The Independent.*

Nelson, Emmanuel S. "Introduction." *Reworlding: The Literature of the Indian Diaspora.* Ed. Emmanuel S. Nelson. New York: Greenwood Press, 1992. ix-xvi.

Nyman, Jopi. "Preface." *The Atlantic Literary Review. Special Issue on Diasporic Indian Fiction.* Vol. 2 No. 4, Oct.-Dec. 2002.

Parameswaran, Uma. "Dispelling the Spells of Memory: Another Approach to Reading our Yesterdays." *Proceedings of the Red River Conference on World Literature.* Vol. 2, 28 Dec. 2002, http://www. ndsu. edu/ RRCWL/V2/Uma. html

Said, Edward. "Interview with Nikhil Padgaonkar." *Doordarshan's Metro Channel*, December 6, 1998.

The Theme of Social Justice in Ann Bhalla's *A Passing Shadow*

13

K.A. Agarwal

Ann Bhalla, as a psychological writer, deals with the theme of cross-culturalism, identity, parent-child relationship and filial sensibility. She has emerged as a new star on the literary firmament with her novels—*A Season For All Things* and *A Passing Shadow*. *A Season For All Things* is an intimate attempt to investigate and explore the cross-cultural relationships. Pascal is the protagonist of the story who is an utter imbroglio "like a sapling uprooted, replanted, and undecided whether to flourish or not in the unfamiliar soil it had been set down in." In her second novel, *A Passing Shadow,* she shows a disaster brought by the insensibility of parents who have been enough to pursue their responsibility.

A Passing Shadow of Ann Bhalla is a novel which is based on the texture of human psychology. Ramesh, the protagonist, encounters Mala. She was deprived of her parental love and care. She leads her life in a missionary school and works in there as a governess to the children of Ramesh. Both are attracted physically to each other and get indulged in sexual affair without having a patch of love on either part.

Ramesh takes her as a time pass entertainment. The sexual attachment makes Mala pregnant. She begins to love this unborn child and so she shows her reluctance for abortion.

Ramesh's wife, Uma is a kind and sympathetic woman. She understands the situation. She proposes the help in marrying Mala with the person she loved, but she does not disclose the name of her lover. Uma is kind enough to make arrangements to send her to her mother who was running a home for the helpless and downtrodden women of the area. Mala after giving birth to a female child dies. Mrs. Bimla Bhushan, who is the mother of Uma, is also very kind and accepts the responsibility to bring up the orphan child and names her Tara. At the age of five Tara loses Mrs. Bimla Bhushan and now she is in charge of Uma. But her real father Ramesh is not happy with his own daughter. The little child appears to Ramesh to be a problem. He doubts that perhaps Tara is not his issue as she does not resemble either his wife or Ramesh himself. He is surprised to see the blue eyes, dark chestnut hair and hazel green doe-sniped eyes of Tara and this rouses hatred against the child:

> A wild hope surged in his breast that Mala had been meeting someone else besides him but it dies away just as quickly. He knew it had not been possible for so many reasons, chief among them that she had been too besotted with him to look at another man. (106)

In the novel there is a parallel character Somnath Prakash living in Springfield, Virginia, who prays in his daily devotion for the well-being of new born babe whom he placed upon the steps of an ancient church. He has his second wife without disclosing her the death of his first wife and having a child from her. He regrets for all this but keeps it as a secret:

> With a helpless feeling of sad resignation, he whispered a last prayer for the child he had abandoned twenty one years ago on a warm summer's day at dawn. It was a short prayer, one that he said everyday of his life since then. He asked God to take care of her wherever she was and begged forgiveness for what he had done. (83)

Both Ramesh and Somnath Prakash are insensible fathers to their children. But there is one little difference between two fathers. Somnath Prakash is a better father than Ramesh. The former abandoned the child because of miserable circumstances but the latter got the child out of his amorous cravings for the sexual pleasure. He is hard hearted and does not regret for his wrong desires. He is also feelingless at the sad demise of his sexual partner, Mala. Moreover, he is inhuman when he feels relieved at the tragic end of Mala. He used her only as a 'use and throw' thing. Mala was purely a temporary pleasure toy for him:

> The fear of exposure no longer threatened him. The dismal dusk of despair that engulfed him for the day that Mala had declared her pregnancy could now be pushed out of his mind. No longer need he worry about renewing his search for a flat or think of fabricated excuses to visit his mistress and their child. He had been reprieved. As Mala had come into his life, she went out of it, a pawn of Fate, a passing shadow. Or so he had believed at the time. (82)

Somnath Prakash, on the other hand, is a kind hearted and nice human being. He repents sincerely for his guilt. He has full sympathy and sincere love for Farida who is Kashmiri Muslim girl, whom he married at the Arya Samaj mandir, and the innocent girl was unfortunately killed on the spot in an accident. His daughter, Mala, was just three days old and Somnath Prakash's parents, being staunch Hindus were not ready to accept the girl child (Mala) because she was a half Muslim child. Somnath Prakash is helpless before his parents but within the core of heart he regrets sincerely. It is his great fault that he does not oppose the injustice of his parents. Moreover, he stoops down before them. He marries second time. Though he is pure at heart but does not have courage to face the problem in a justified way. The circumstances for him were not easy to handle but he has deep sense of regret and thinks that he is not blessed again with a child through his second marriage because it was God's way of punishing him for what he had done. He does not want to disclose this secret to his wife.

He always lives in the shadow of his sin and never forgets about his child. After the death of his wife he makes resolution to trace the whereabout of his lost daughter, Mala. It shows his purity of heart. But, on the other hand, Ramesh is not ready at any case to reveal his weakness of his character to his wife Uma. His son Anand falls in love with Mala's daughter Tara. Ramesh is shocked to know it and he finds himself to control him and discontinue his affairs with Tara. At last he resolves to reveal Anand the fact of Tara and also wants to tell him that she is his sister. Before this incident we find ironical aspect of his personality. He has no love for his daughter, Tara. He has no sympathy even with his own blood and in spite of repeated request of his wife, Uma, to show some sparks of love and emotion to Tara because she is not responsible for her parent's misdeeds; he loses his temper and uses harsh words even against his wife:

> Why do you always stand up for her? She has her mother's blood running in her veins and all know what her mother was—an immoral little bitch. "I didn't know it", Uma said, "How do you know she was?" He had quickly backtracked.
>
> Actions speak louder than words. How do you suppose she brought an illegitimate child into the world? A child who seems to have inherited the same trait, judging from the way she lured Anand into their affairs. (282)

We find the climax of the story in part IV Dawn. Anand is aware about the real father of Tara and even Ramesh does not dare to discourage the truth. Anand is the elder son of Ramesh and has deep love for Tara. He shows adamantly his intention to marry Tara. At last Ramesh is forced to tell him the reason to withhold his permission for it is incestuous marriage. Ramesh reveals Anand the fact why he has been trying to stop him to marry Tara:

> "Tara is your half sister, Anand. That is why you cannot marry her."
>
> "You mean an adopted sister, didn't you? It's not the same thing as half sister."
>
> "I know the difference Anand. She is your half sister. I am" he paused, gulped and could not bring out the words 'her father'. "I had a brief affair with her mother and she is the result." (286-87)

Anand is shocked to know the real character of his father whom he used to consider a man of high character, but this fact shatters his very high notions about him. He thinks that his outward personality is so nice but he is astonished to see his inner self so mischievous:

> My God: Is that all you can think of? How could you have lived for more than twenty years deceiving her,

> deceiving all of us, especially Tara? Treating her the way you did? Your own daughter. (288)

Ann Bhalla in her novel depicts the parents-child relationship, suffering from the blows of insensibility from time to time. There is a great psychological conflict in the minds of the son and the father. On the one hand, Anand is badly hurt to know the reality of the birth of his beloved. He is neither in a position to marry her nor to leave her love; while on the other hand, his father considers his wife, Uma, responsible for all this trouble. He blames her responsible for this disharmony in the family because she is the cause to get Tara into the house. Anand loses his temper and bursts out:

> "You always throw the blame for your actions on someone else." Anand said bitterly. "What did you plan on doing then? Put your own child into some unknown orphanage?... Did you have no shame? No decency." (288)

Anand begins to hate his irresponsible father. But he does not want to punish him for his sin. His marriage with Tara was out of question. He is torn within his own self and consequently commits suicide as under these circumstances. He leaves a suicide note and blames nobody for his death. Anand is a sincere young lover. Unlike his father he neither cheats his beloved nor wants to make her life a hell. In his suicide note he advises Tara to marry a man of her choice and forget him forever. He also tells that he could not live without getting her in marriage but now it was not possible after knowing the fact. Moreover, he cannot go through the pain of seeing her eventually marrying someone else nor can he allow her to remain unmarried because of him. But if he leaves this world, perhaps she will in time find another man to love and lean on. It is the psychological fact that the children love and feel attached to their parents throughout their lives. Moreover, in the childhood their parents look after their health and fulfill their basic needs.

The parents are most respectable for them but the moment the sense of dignity in parents is gone, the filial bond becomes weak. In Ann Bhalla's novel *A Passing Shadow,* the male characters are irresponsible but on the other hand, the female characters are full of love, affection, and are sincere to their off-springs. In the novel, female characters like Bimla Bhushan, mother of Uma, Uma herself, Farida and even Mala have never been insensible towards the children.

Tara does not pay any regard to Ramesh and dislikes him, but she has a deep respect for Uma, who has been very affectionate to her just like a mother. This was only her compassionate nature that Tara could grow up in the family in spite of indifference of Ramesh. She was provided not only family protection but good education also for the better prospects of her life. Uma has always a sense of belongingness to Tara but we find that her own father Ramesh has no love or belongingness for her. So Tara has negative feelings against her father. She has no love or respect for Ramesh. The insensibility of Somnath Prakash led to disaster in Shanti Niwas. The novelist wants to stress that illicit love always causes enough problems to destroy many lives and the same we find in the case of Ramesh. His illicit love is the root cause of the dark shadows in the life of Tara. Ann Bhalla tells that conjugal love is a nectar in the lives of husband and wife, outside this love is a cause of obstruction in the family.

WORK CITED

Bhalla, Ann. *A Passing Shadow*. New Delhi: Ocean Books, 2002. (All the references have been from this edition.)

Cultural Discordance: A Study of Diasporic Writers in Canada

14

Samina Khan

The presence of two cultures in one's mind forms a wider and saner basis on which the quest for identity originates. This presence also gives birth to a kind of discordance which is sometimes confusing and sometimes creative. B. Rajan suggests that "man with mixed allegiances is contemporary 'Everyman'..."

Fortunately Canada and India are bound together by more than one bond. Both the nations are freedom loving; both have a past of colonial experience; and both are now busy in building themselves as the two sovereign democratic countries, with immense possibilities of cultural and educational expansion. Besides these common features, there are many other features which are different in both the countries. This presence of two cultures has been studied in some of the writers of Indian diaspora in Canada. The study includes Balachandra Rajan, Cowasjee among the novelists and Tilottama Rajan and Uma Parameswaran among the poets, living presently in Canada. The study of these authors shows the cultural contact and interaction between Canada and India. They emerge as the potent messengers of Indian thought and culture to a distant land of the West.

Challenges of Diversity: A Study of Diasporic Writers in Canada

As the title itself unfolds, the present attempt is a study of some Indian authors like Balachandra Rajan and, Saros Cowasjee, among the novelists and Tilottama Rajan and Uma Parameswaran among the poets, living currently in Canada, perhaps, permanently. This attempt precludes the critical corpus of these selected authors. Who does not know that B. Rajan is an established critic on Milton and Yeats and Eliot, that Saros

Cowasjee and Uma Parameswaran are well-known Indian scholars, and that Tilottama Rajan is the 'Preconcious' (Iyengar 83) child of a reputed author? Taken together, these authors serve as a strong chain in the cultural interaction of India and Canada, the two loving partners in the Commonwealth.

As stated above, B. Rajan is a reputed literary figure who has produced two novels entitled *The Dark Dancer* (1985) and *Too Long in the West* (1961). In these novels, Rajan is acutely conscious of "the presence of two cultures" of the East and the West. As Rajan himself states in his article *Identity and Nationality:*

> ...the presence of two cultures in one's mind forms a wider and therefore saner basis on which too originates the quest for identity, and...the discordance between these two cultures can be creative as well as merely confusing. Perhaps one can go further and suggest that the man with mixed allegiances is contemporary 'Everyman'.... (108)

Through this statement, Rajan has clarified his own position obliquely—that he is a "contemporary Everyman" of "mixed allegiances". It is nothing surprising to one who is fully acquainted with his background—that he was born and bred in India, educated in Cambridge, and taught with distinction as Professor of English in at least three countries—England, India and Canada—and wrote a number of standard books, and finally settled down at Toronto in Canada. His two novels are remarkable studies in cross-cultural contact between the East and the West, as a brief summary of them will clearly demonstrate.

The Dark Dancer throws up a series of swift changes and challenges in the life of V.S. Krishnan, a Cambridge trained personality. After completing his higher education in Cambridge, Krishnan returns to India to be caged in an arranged marriage with Kamala, an M.A. in Sanskrit and a sober girl by nature. He joins the Government Secretariat in New Delhi, and meets incidentally his old girl-friend Cynthia Brainbird in a club and dances with her. Meanwhile, Kamala has to go to the South to see her ailing mother, promising to return in fortnight. On her return, she discovers Krishnan's deep attachment to Cynthia, and her husband admits it. One day, Kamala slips away to Shantipur without telling anyone, but Vijayaraghavan (Krishnan's friend) locates her. Krishnan, who has by now severed his relationship with Cynthia, visits Shantipur to find Kamala. Kamala is presently an altered person, with a mission in life. In the wake of Indian independence, riots break out everywhere, even in the small town of Shantipur, resulting in horrors of mass-killing, looting, arson and rape. The wisdom of the Medical Officer, Kamala and Krishnan brings the widespread cholera under control. Kamala is, however, attacked by two drunkards with a sharp-edged knife and a *lethal lathi* in one of her evening walks, and she dies within no time. Krishnan is also badly injured in trying to safeguard his wife. The drunkards are immediately lynched to death by the irate mob. After ten days, Krishnan comes out of the trauma of assault and leaves for Benaras to immerse his wife's ashes into the holy Ganges there. He also performs all the rites ordained by the *Shastras* under the supervision of Kruger and his parents and father-in-law (Shankaran). His mother talks of his remarriage, but he coldly snubs her saying, "I'll stay single...God knows I've made enough mistake" (The Dark Dancer 301). Krishnan is now totally transformed, living as he does with Kamala's memories—and Kamala had died a gallant death in rescuing a Muslim girl from the clutches of the two brats—and deriving consolation from the *Bhagavad Gita*. This personal transformation of Krishnan is confirmed by his rejection of Cynthia who re-appears after the death of Kamala. Krishnan advises her: "Go home and settle for ninety-eight per cent" (305). The cultural ambivalence is clearly witnessed here in the form of Kamala and Cynthia. Thus *The Dark Dancer* is an intense story of the self-division and maturation of an individual and of a nation, of the cyclic phenomenon of fratricidal war and its message transmitted in the blood-consciousness of people.

"*Too Long in the West* is a hilarious comedy, a spoof of the absurdities in Indian and American social codes, of arranged marriage, and of the foibles and eccentricities of individuals"

(Parameswaran 125). Nalini, the heroine, is the only daughter of Sambasivan and Laksmi. She has been to Columbia in America for higher studies and returns to India, to the hazards of her father's village called Mudalur after her long stay in the West. Her father has already advertised her prospective marriage in newspapers, to which the correct yet miserable Satyamurthy, the phenomenologist Kaliyansundaram, the handsome and prosperous Kubera, the stiff and stubborn Vishwakarman, and American chummy Earnest Hamilton Jones, have favorably responded. They are comforted at Hailview, the residence of Sambasivan after the village barber Raman, a barbarous and blood-thirsty fellow, arrives there and incites the whole hamlet against the Sambasivan family. He is particularly against the intimacy of 'Nalini with Earnest Jones'. The villagers approach Sambasivan and threaten him to send off his daughter in marriage by the next morning or to face the dire consequences. As a result, a sort of *swayamvara* (self-selection of the groom) is arranged, and to the amazement of all Nalini selects Raman as her life-partner, pursuing the policy—"if you cannot lick'em goin'em" (*Too Long in the West* 187). This might be a wise tactical move on the part of Nalini to appease a turbulent man, but aesthetically this is the least satisfying. Subsequently, the bully Raman takes to the task of a nose-and-ear piercer of ladies. Nalini was forewarned by Kalyani in the train about the kind of situation she was to face in Indian society: "you won't fit in...you'll always be an exile and an alien, a self created foreigner refugee from yourself. You can't belong. You'll live in two worlds and fall between two stools" (55). The novel under review unfurls cultural interaction between the East and the West through the heroine Nalini and the anonymous writer for the *Times Literary Supplement* judiciously observes that this novel is "a story about the class of Indian and American cultures" (Anonymous *TLS* 313).

Another Indian novelist of light weight is Saros Cowasjee, a professor of English at the University of Ragina in Canada, who has written a novel titled *Goodbye to Elsa* (1974), besides his critical studies on the major fiction of Dr. Mulk Raj Anand. *Goodbye to Elsa* is largely a love tale, recounting the adventures of its one-eyed protagonist called Tristan Elliot, an Anglo-Indian by birth and British by education. After his sad experiences in Delhi, fatherless as he was though his careful mother was still alive, he joined the Indian Army as an officer on the recommendations of Col. Ross and resigned out of his own accord. He made love to beautiful Nellie for a while and left for Dublin, then "for Leeds and London, on her departure to Bombay when she met a train accident and lost her legs. He did complete his Ph.D. on Henry II in History from the University of Leeds, but not before undergoing the harrowing experiences of love and sex with such diverse women as Jane, Lydia, deceptive Heather Malleson, and Elsa Harbour (whom he ultimately married and by whom he had a one-year-old son). But he didn't like Elsa for her heavy weight (of 180 pounds), and tried to contact some other women like Julia (who refused to oblige him) and Lily (a whore, with whom he couldn't get on)" (118). On the recommendations of his Supervisor, Dr. Adams, he was given a suitable teaching job at Erigon in Canada, and Elsa persuaded him to buy the old house of Prof. Peabody. Soon he developed a burning eye sore in his left eye, which couldn't be saved. Two week afterwards, he left his house, his wife and son behind, and went straight to the Army and Navy store to purchase a .22 rifle and a thousand cartridges, with the intention of killing himself in the North at the Mountain View in Corwind. Meanwhile, Tristan got hungry and walked down a long distance to reach a store of groceries, where he made some purchases but couldn't get a few items of daily use. So, he left his address with the grocer, who sent one of his daughters called Marie to him with the required supply. An intense affair sprang between them, and they decided to get married soon. For her sake, he gave up the idea of slaying himself and started leading a life of renewed zeal. She also had to shift to Vancouver for a book-keeping job, with the promise that she would invite him as soon as she found a spacious room for two. But Marie met her boyfriend Joe there and changed her mind of marrying Tristan. She informed him accordingly in a letter. Now, Tristan grew revengeful, went out to the grocer, 'brought back Marie's sister, Marison', who is equally young and charming, and shot her dead when she attempted to escape, and got ready to kill himself then and thereafter ringing his wife and bidding her "goodbye". Though the novel is primarily concerned with women and wine in the life of Tristan, the protagonist, the scene keeps shifting swiftly from Canada to India and to England and back to Canada in a cinematic fashion. The novelist has offered us vignettes of life in these various countries as well as of the persons and places in Canadian cities like Erigon, Corwind, Vancouver and Toronto. He occasionally throws light on the ways of behaviour and conduct of Canadians in the course of his novel, such as when Dr. Adams remarks: "it is a fairly civilized place. You will find all the amenities of like life there..." (89) and when Tristan observes thus: "Besides, the Canadians are so neutral, they are neither sane nor insane, good or bad. They generally take the colour from their surroundings" (42). Cowasjee also betrays his consciousness of the independent 'nationality' and 'identity' of Canada vis-a-vis the USA and shrewdly comments: "We have to be on the guard all the time against the Americanization of Canada. It is a matter of preserving our Canadian identity" (117).

Tilottama Rajan studied at the Ontario University, Canada, where her illustrious father lectured, and published a poetic collection under the caption *Myth in a Metal Mirror* in 1967, when she was barely sixteen. This collection contains 36 poems in all, and is divided into three sections, the first section having 21 poems; the second 5 icons and the third 14 poems. Of the three, the third one is more experimental in art and technique and yet more erratic in expression than the first two. These sections are preceded by an illuminating four-page Introduction where Tilottama makes some sensible statements about *Subjectivity* and *Typography*. Here she states that a poet "does not express an objective reality through symbols" but "creates with the symbols a subjective reality which is cold and clinical or dark and unpredictable as the case may be" (Introduction *Myth in a Metal Mirror*). Tilottama remarks further that all existence is "an optical translation", and each individual object is thus "progressively subjectivised". And that modern art "can provide a poet with something lacking in poetry and present a sense of the poem as an original source; a primal energy!" The young poetess ends her *Introduction* by pointing out that a poet should create "a definite sense of individuality", which usually comes from "a persistent image or metaphor, from the use of shock tactics (as in, cumuning's case) or from the introduction of techniques suggested by such popular industries as the film industry or advertising". In Miss Rajan's poetry, the reader comes across such insistent images as the dark sun, the mirror, the camera, and the human eye (i.e., the mind). One of the most significant poems in her collection is "Lies" (in section I), which offers us the following extracts:

> The eye is in the room
> Breaking and twisting objects
> Into 'legendary shapes'. (15)

and

> Shield of steel turning
> Through a myth
> The artificial sun lies in the sky
> Shield of the steel burning
> Through a Myth. (16)

The age-old myths are looked upon as the twisted reflections in a modern steel or metal mirror. Miss Rajan's poetical volume shows unmistakable traces of T.S. Eliot and B. Rajan who had also written a long poem, *Damayanti,* in his younger days. There are at least two pieces on the making of 'Poem' in it.

Another Indian poetess is Uma Parameswaran, who is a professor of English at the University of Winnipeg in Canada. Her poetical volume, *Cyclic Hope Cyclic Pain,* appeared in 1973 from the Writers Workshop (like Tilottama's). Consisting of barely nine poems and a dance-drama entitled "Meera" it has poems without captions; only numbers are given. The poems are emotionally surcharged, as she largely dwells on the intimate experiences of a mother. Right from the day of conception to the day of the child's birth, the mother experiences 'cyclic hope and cyclic pain'. The opening poem subtly depicts the meeting of lovers in a 'dark chamber', and the second one reveals the 'urgency', of purpose, especially in the lines:

The sun came fiery white,
Afraid. I received him
With a prism. (2)

All the pains and sorrows of the mother disappear with the birth of a lovely son who gives out his first cry of 'Ma'. This can be easily inferred from the following passage:

And I said
This will pass'
And one day I will know
The joys of ripened motherhood
The joys of being mother of man. (Ma 9-10)

At the close of the poem, the same son having grown up approaches the mother for her blessings while leaving her for better prospects and academic distinctions. With a heavy heart the mother blesses him and informs him of her last wish—that he should set fire to her 'funeral pyre'. So far as "Meera" is concerned, it was produced and directed by Rubena Sinha for the Hindu Society of Manitoba on April 2, 1972. Running into nine pages, "Meera" consists of five short scenes, all related to the life of the central character in it. Meera is married to Prince Bhoja, who expires prematurely. His brother succeeds him, but hates Meera from the core of his heart; as she is frantically devoted to Lord Krishna—and is a "handmaid of Lord Krishna now and forever" (*Cyclic Hope Cyclic Pain*). At the close of the dance-drama, Meera assumes the role of Radha, and Krishna joins her far leaving behind the gossip in an ecstatical dance of creation. This dance-drama is nearly of the size of a one-act play and is undoubtedly packed with passion, pulse and power.

To conclude, the four Indian authors studied here sufficiently show the cultural contact and interaction between India and Canada. They emerge as the potent messengers of the Indian thought and culture to a distant land of the West. Fortunately, India and Canada are bound together by more than one bond. Both the nations are freedom-loving; both have had a past of colonial experience; and both are now busy in building themselves as the two sovereign democratic republics, with the immense possibilities of cultural and educational expansion. They have learnt enough by now to tread on the path of equality and fraternity, and they have no dangers of coercion or intimidation in their bilateral and international relationships. A cultural interaction between them has ensured greater understanding and closeness between them.

WORKS CITED

Anonymous. "Indian Ink." *The Times Literary Supplement,* 19th May, 1961.

Cowasjee, Saros. *Goodbye to Elsa.* The Bodley Head, London: Sydney and Toronto, 1974.

Iyengar, K.R. Srinivasa. *Indian Writing in English.* New Delhi: Sterling Publishers Pvt. Ltd., 1984.

Parameswaran, Uma. *A Study of Representative Indo-English Novelists.* New Delhi: Vikas Publishing House Pvt. Ltd., 1976.

——. *Cyclic Hope Cyclic Pain.* Calcutta: Writers Workshop, 1973.

Rajan, B. "Identity and Nationality." *Commonwealth Literature.* Ed. John Press, London: Heinemann Educational Books, 1965.

——. *The Dark Dancer.* New Delhi: Arnold Heinemann Publishers India Ltd., 1976.

——. *Too Long in the West.* Bombay: Jaico Publishing House, 1961.

Rajan, Tilottama. "Introduction." *Myth in a Metal Mirror.* Calcutta Shop, 1967.

15

Across Cultures Discussing Yasmine Gooneratne's *Masterpiece*

Sangeeta Das

Yasmine Gooneratne, a Sri Lankan born Australian writer, having no definite perspective of rich Indian culture, just heard a story about the life of a Sanskrit poet from her Indian colleague and could not be left bereft of the ever engulfing influence of the great Indian culture. She was greatly intrigued by the story of Jayadeva and his bold attempt to literally present the symbolic gesture of victory in their erotic play imagined by him. Though Jayadeva could not complete his play himself treading on such tentative grounds, Lord Krishna himself had to come down to complete it. Selection of this theme by Yasmine Gooneratne justifies the fact that no-matter wherever one may be born and brought up, one's imaginations and thoughts know no boundaries and flies across the wide oceans and seas and investigates unhindered the cultures of lands, known and unknown. Yasmine Gooneratne has also indicated a cross-cultural ease that underlies her delightful wit and urbanity. In her two novels, *A Change of Sky* (1992) and *Pleasure of Conquest* (1995) she had explored at length the comic possibilities of the experience of dislocation and some not so comic consequences of post-colonial mobility. As an academic she may theorise about migration and diaspora, but as a fiction writer she deals with specific situations vividly, without explicit judgement, sometimes assumed at the absurdities produced by the mismatch of cultural assumptions, at other times anguished at hostilities, that waste human lives.

In this grand story *Masterpiece* which rightly justifies the title, the author recounts the tale which she had heard from an Indian colleague during a train journey. This masterpiece which happened to be the *Gita Govinda* created nine centuries ago, is called as *The Song of the Shepherd* in the West. This masterpiece deals with the love of God Krishna for Radha, the herd-girl. The Indian colleague of Yasmine Gooneratne recounts the story as discussed in the seminar in which he happened to be invited. The subject chosen to be discussed in the seminar was *Gita Govinda* itself, its status in relation to India's classical heritage and to world literature, its literary qualities and the process of its composition. Taking into account the composition of the *Masterpiece*, a well-known storyteller of the region was asked to speak in the seminar. The narration of the composition of the *Masterpiece* and interaction between the storyteller and the Australian professor throws light on the difference in thoughts, beliefs, cultures and progress between the two countries.

We must not forget that the *Masterpiece* was written in the 12th century when the social stratification was vastly different than what it is today. Old people upheld the old social set-up and looked down upon the progressive development of recent times. In those days, women were like decoration pieces to be treasured and kept, confined in the house. Their education was unnecessary. Their qualification was how good they could serve their husbands who used to be double of their age. Dedication to housework and on toes in serving their husbands was the grid on which the suitability of a girl was gauged. This advantage was enjoyed by Jayadeva, the Sanskrit poet who wrote the *Masterpiece* and was the hero of the story. He had a complaisant wife who never argued with him and served him diligently over the days considering her husband's success as her own thus facilitating Jayadeva to reach smoothly to the completion of his work. The Australian professor who had come on visiting appointment in Delhi and had got just married was quite impressed with Indian women especially with the endurance and docility of Jayadeva's wife.

Credibility and eminence of Jayadeva was never questioned or doubted either in the 12th century or today. We Indians have great deference for our Gods, Goddesses and the literati who have written many great pieces like *Mahabharata*, *Ramayana*, *Gita Govinda* etc. Nobody ever dare refute these great people and their works. Both the works and their composers are intricately and intimately attached to our sentiments. Knowing that Indians are sentimental and emotional both, any encroachment in that direction was sure to be met with irritation and intolerance. Such instance can be seen in the conversation between the story-teller and the Australian professor.

When Jayadeva got stuck in the midst of his writing, the story-teller had no reason to put before for such a clog while the Australian professor came up with a practical reason of 'Writer's Block' which usually happens to a writer while writing. This was strongly refuted by the story-teller for Jayadeva was not any just writer but a writer of genius and geniuses never encounter the flaws faced by ordinary men. He should be looked upon with reverence as he had done a masterpiece upholding the Indian culture and surely couldn't have been able to do so without divine blessings. The story-teller's irritation towards the professor was evidence enough of the staunch credulity of Indians for their scholars.

Too much interest shown towards the poet's wife by the professor was also met with bitter rebuff by the story-teller. The professor was plainly mesmerized by the obedience and compatibility of the wife and having married an Indian girl was filled with happy expectations of receiving such a pleasant demeanour from his wife. His inquisitiveness was nothing but appreciation for the lady's endurance and acceptance of her husband's progress and consequent success.

The most ironical and depressing revelation comes when after so much devotion, subservience and endurance, she receives doubt on her fidelity by her husband just because the poem was completed by someone else, in his absence. This doubt reined so high on his mind that he could not rejoice over the completion of the poem. His wife, in turn, was intensely pained and took him to the temple where an ink stain on the finger of Lord Krishna established the fact that it was God Krishna who had come disguised as Jayadeva, ate his meal and completed the poem. The point not to be overlooked in the story is the utter vulnerability of a woman's identity and credibility in our society. She was not only kept uneducated but also expected to be homely, i.e. good in household work and serve her husband as best as possible, in return, she was constantly in danger of being emotionally and mentally exploited. The wife had a great heart and forgave her husband whom she placed next to God.

The idea of a woman put above a man was excessively objectionable and terrifying to the story-teller. This was evident when the professor suggested an alternative interpretation to the conclusion of the poem. Interpretation was quite practical viewing the circumstances.

The poet's wife was sad to see her husband's hunch of despair and may be to ease his trouble she had made an attempt at completing the poem. This interpretation of the poet was vehemently opposed by the story-teller. He not only admonished the professor for having woman in his mind but also condemned him of sacrilege. He found the whole idea totally ridiculous and impossible as a respectable woman of 12th century never had any association with palm leaf and stylus. The concept of woman education was extremely unacceptable in those days and no man of senses would marry a girl who could read and write. Looking back to those days, we Indian women of today surely feel ourselves lucky and fortunate. In stark contrast, no man of sense, today would marry a girl who could not read and write. Nine centuries gap has turned the tables and has changed the social scenario completely. The dilemma of the professor is quite natural and justified. He belonged to 21st century and the story-teller was the spokesperson of 12th century. There had to be a cultural and thematic clash between them. The concept of 'homely' itself varies between India and Australia. In India, homely means a woman besides attractive should be good at household works whereas the professor believed that 'homely' meant a plain and simple looking woman. Beauty and attraction was secondary. Expertise at household work was given priority.

Though the story-teller has repeatedly stressed that the story dealt with Jayadeva and his masterpiece and not with influence of women or men, but his antagonism over professor's indication of the poet's wife, completing the work and consequently threatening him with not giving too much precedence to his wife for a happy married life, does not enhance the position of man in our eyes rather leaves a bad taste by ignoring the sacrifice of a wife for her husband's success.

Yasmine Gooneratne may have been wonder-struck with immense capabilities of scholars in India with their endurance and perseverance under stringent circumstances but could not have overlooked the indifference and silent ignorance of the equal contribution of women in their husband's work.

While Jayadeva deals with Lord Krishna's boundless love for Radha, he strangely ignores the silent and deep love of his wife for himself. How can a man, dealing with such an elevated theme in his work which turned out to be a masterpiece, could remain immune to so much love and devotion in his personal life? Jayadeva's greatness is shadowed to some extent by his doubt for his wife's fidelity who has been shown to have only his happiness uppermost on her mind.

Our culture may be very rich and immense but such ignorance and indifference towards woman in a country of rich heritage before an Australian professor who had all appreciation and sympathy for the wife, conveniently forgotten, fills me with shame. A foreigner has the eyes to see the greatness which we Indians have always failed to notice and acknowledge.

I don't know exactly what Yasmine Gooneratne had in mind when she recounted the story but through the professor I can get glimpse of regions where women have an identity of their own.

WORK CITED

Gooneratne, Yasmine. *Masterpiece.* New Delhi: India Law Publications Pvt. Ltd., 2002.

Bicultural Sensibility: A Motif in Divakaruni's *The Unknown Errors of Our Lives* 16

Beena Agarwal

In the wake of globalisation, the writers of Indian Diaspora have set a distinctive trend of fictional perspective. Their writings represent an uncompromising quest for the native cultural heritage with the longing for the assimilation in alien culture and it subsequently prepares a fine fabric of human sensitivity and relationship hitherto unknown in the realm of Indian fiction. Chitra Banerjee Divakaruni with the strength of her narrative skill captures the crucial moments of life at the crossroad moments—caught between past and present, excitement for the West and the longing for East, along with the conflict of tradition and modernity. Untainted by the compulsions of established authority or the pretension of artistic excellence, Divakaruni in her collection of short stories *The Unknown Errors of Our Lives* (2001), vitalises the apathy of the life of those who have to witness the crisis of 'homeland' and 'hostland'. Junot Diaz rightly remarks as marked on the jacket of the text:

> A current of compassion and heartache runs through this remarkable collection—from old immigrant conundrums, Divakaruni has spun something wondrous and new; she has created the stories that we will require in the age of Diasporas.

The exceptional sensibility about the drama of human emotions, geographical locations affecting the pattern of familial and interpersonal relationship, the tendency of preaching the common codes of life against the vanity of West imparts her a distinctive identity among the writers of Indian diaspora. Like Bharati Mukherjee, Divakaruni's celebration of Indian soul and soil, is not a romantic nostalgia but a realisation of life itself. It results in the split of psyche, torn between the conflicting pull of ideals—individual and society, personal and familial, past and present, reality and illusion. These seeming contradictions prepare a pattern of life experiences in the stories conceived by Divakaruni. Ha Jin appreciates her as marked on the jacket of the text:

> This is an extraordinary collection, intelligently conceived and passionately written. The stories illuminate the pain, loss and alienation of the immigrant experience and transform them into the drama of our common human existence. Besides elegance and delight, we can also find wisdom here.

In the text of the writers of diaspora, the quest for identity in their homeland and the land of their adoption has been a focal point of speculation. The crisis springs out of the clash of socio-psychic affinity with the native culture and the new bonds of affinity with new culture. The cumulative effect of geographical locations, separation from cultural roots and a detachment from tradition, motivates a "fractured psyche" affecting the balance of the personality. Henry B. Wonham has pointed out that literary creativity depends on the unconscious accumulation of local knowledge. Berry Lopez commenting upon "A Literature of Place" writes:

> I want to talk geography as a shaping force, not a subject...a specific and particular setting of human experience and endeavour is, indeed central to work of many nature writers, I would say a sense of place is also critical to the development of a sense of morality and of human identity. (7)

The terms "exile", "rootlessness", "displacement" and "alienation" are partially judicious to communicate the sensibility of expatriates but they can't elucidate the visible and invisible impressions working on the inner psyche of the characters. The process of assimilation requires the forgetting of 'past' but the absolute negation of 'past' is difficult to achieve because the lingering shadows of past persistently interact with the present and hinder the process of assimilation. Expatriation sensibility involves social assimilation and the reconstruction of psychic self. To quote:

> Expatriation is actually a complex state of mind and emotion which includes a wistful longing for the past, often symbolised by ancestral home, the pain of exile and homelessness, the struggle to maintain the differences between oneself and the new unfriendly surroundings, as assumption of moral and cultural superiority over the host country and a refusal to accept the identity forced one of the environment. The expatriate builts a cocoon around herself/himself or refuses from cultural dilemma and from the experienced hostility or unfriendliness in the new country. (Gomez 72)

The agony of migrancy depends on the level of education, age and the motive behind migration. Neither the dislocation nor absorption can be total, "Physical dislocation is not the only dislocation and the levels of affluence not the only determinant" (Introduction by Jain 17). George Steiner describes the expatriate writer as the "contemporary everyman".

In the shorter fiction of Chitra Banerjee Divakaruni, the pain of exile has been exposed through the protagonists who are nostalgic for the past and in absence of any amicable solution, they compromise with the real life conditions. The self-preservation and self-realisation of Divakaruni's protagonists involve the consistent flux of memories between past and present, between homeland and hostland, between glamour of the West and peace of the East. Such characters often share the anguish of their own creators and such emotional affinity between the character and creator imparts a rare quality of self-revelation and self-preservation. Jasbir Jain in her article *Geographical Dislocation and the Poetics of Exile: Ashis Gupta and Michel Ondaatje* describes these expatriates:

> Writers who have moved away from one culture to another are caught between two cultures and are very often engaged either in a process of self-recovery through resort to history and memory or in a process of self-preservation through an act of transformation. (Jain 101)

In the nine prominent stories in the collection *The Unknown Errors of Our Lives*—"Mrs. Dutta Writes a Letter", "The Intelligence of Wild Things", "The Lives of Strangers", "The Love of a Good Man", "What the Body Knows", "The Forgotten Children", The Blooming Season for Cacti", "The Unknown Errors of our Lives" and "The Names of Stars in Bengali"—Divakaruni expresses her sentimental concern for the changing pattern of familial relationship in the process of migration. The geographical shift of location reshapes the fabric of human relationship and subsequently contributes to a new meaning in life. Divakaruni admits that 'rootlessness' is not hidden in the shift of location but in the distortion of the images of human life.

The story "Mrs. Dutta Writes a Letter" is a pathetic account of the experiences of an immigrant woman who resists the forces of patriarchy and the trauma of immigration simultaneously. Divakaruni's argument is that a woman as a migrant is doubly marginalised, struggling against the horrors of immigration and the apathy of gender discrimination. Mrs. Dutta, an elderly widow from a traditional Bengali family, migrates to America to stay in the family of her son, Sagar and daughter-in-law Shyamoli. In the family of her son, her simple habits were looked down. Once she fixes 'Alarm' in the clock because she was taught by her mother-in-law that a "good housewife wakes before the rest of the household". However, both Sagar and Shyamoli contemptuously criticise her. Divakaruni is conscious to decode the sensitivity of "divided self" of immigrants through the web of familial relationship. Sagar consoles his mother, "We want you to be comfortable, Ma. To rest. That's why we brought you to America" (3) but irony is implicit in his illusion of reality. She was not permitted to survive according to her own choices. Even the habits like early rising and chanting of *Mantra* were a hurdle in the routine of Sagar and Shyamoli. For them *Mantra* instead of being the celebration of divine reverence was criticized to distract their peace of mind. Mrs. Dutta gets a letter from her friend Mrs. Basu who enquires, "Are you happy in America?" This idea of "happiness" gives a jerk to her conscience, compels her to speculate the past in comparison of present. She makes a scanning of the dreams of life in America and the commitments of life in Calcutta. The delicious taste of 'Rasgulla' and 'Alu Dam' haunts her. In Divakaruni's fictional world, Calcutta is not a sign of homeland but a manifesto of the way of life, integrated in individual's conscience and the separation from it involves the complete collapse of personality. Mrs. Dutta does not appreciate Shyamoli's casual attitude towards the management of food. In Indian society, food is not a matter of 'proteins' and 'fats' but a metaphor of 'family' closely related with traditions, habits, sentiments and warmth of personal relations. Dimple, the protagonist of Bharati Mukherjee's celebrated novel *Wife,* is restless in America to drink specific *Darjeeling* Tea. And Mrs. Dutta in the present story makes a desperate comment, "At least the family's eating well since, I arrived,...proper Indian food" (9). After the nostalgia for Indian food, she expresses her longing for the company of her grandchildren. She feels a sense of loss because no one is "waiting in impatient exasperation for her to take on her duties again" (11). For her the company of grandchildren was not a consolation but the pain of reality existing in American society becomes poignant, "they're flesh of my flesh, blood of my blood.... But sometimes when she listens, from the other room, to them speaking on the phone, their American voices rising in excitement as they discuss a glittering alien world of Power Rangers, Spice Girls and Spirit Week at school, she almost cannot believe it" (13). The reactions of Shyamoli and Mrs. Dutta, represent the difference of the responses of two generations—Mrs. Dutta, the first generation of home-seekers, suffers with a sense of loss; Shyamoli, the second generation is looking forward for assimilation. In her responses, there is a reflection of sublimation and rationalisation. In spite of being a young Hindu wife, Shyamoli appreciates that in American society, there is no distinction between 'man's work or woman's work'. She accuses her mother-in-law, "That's why Indian men are so useless around the house. Here in America we don't believe in men's work and women's work" (15). In Mrs. Dutta's life, Sagar's company was the only consolation but she was still not ready to get rid of her past. The lack of emotional satisfaction in the company of Sagar, was a serious vacuum in the life of Mrs. Dutta. He remains busy in office work and spares no time to gossip with his mother. In her letter to Mrs. Basu, she confesses that the real problem lies in her will, her helplessness to mould herself into the American way of life. Her letter is both a self-revelation and self-confession like the monologues of Browning. She confesses:

> I cannot answer your question about whether I am happy, for I am no longer sure I know what happiness is. All I know is that it isn't what I thought it to be. It isn't about being needed. It isn't about being with family either. It has something to do with love. I still think that, but in a different way than I believed earlier, a way I don't have the words to explain. (33)

The anguish of Mrs. Dutta is the manifestation of the psyche of loss. Divakaruni's sympathy with the sense of 'loss' in the life of immigrants has come close to the realisation of Bharati Mukherjee. In one of her stories she admits that the experiences of immigrants represent the discontinuity between the "wish" and "wished for" and in that she finds the sense of betrayal. "It is the tyranny of the American dream that scares me. First you don't exist. Then you are invisible. Then you are funny. Then you are disgusting. Insult is a kind of acceptance" (Mukherjee 26).

In the story "The Intelligence of Wild Things", Divakaruni with intense emotional content and heart rendering realisation of the anguish for familial relationship, establishes how immigration casts its shadows on the warmth of relationship. The narrator is a young married lady who tries to unveil her past through the present of her brother, Tarun. He is settled in Vermont in States. Tarun with his shift to America, leaves behind the sympathy for the homeland, the ailing mother and adventurous childhood. Narrator identifies herself with the suffering of her ailing mother whose only mission in life is "seeing my children before I die". With such confession, Divakaruni affirms that in Indian society, personal relationships are associated with the survival. The narration in the story begins with the description of her trip to her brother Tarun across a frozen lake. She comes to America to discover the reasons of the apathy of Tarun for her native soil and ailing mother. Immediately after arrival, she looks at the framed photograph of a girl who was wearing a T-shirt and Jeans. The idea of friendship with a white girl in America shakes her genuine sensibility for Bengali tradition. She astonishes, "Your girl friend,...you never told me, you had a girl friend especially a white one" (37). She is so prejudiced that she refuses even to sleep on the bed that had already been used by his girl friend, "I saw girl's red hair spread over the pillow. Her pale arms tight around my brother's brown back" (38) To escape the filth of the present of Tarun's life, she reconstructs the joys of childhood excitement, passed in the company of her brother and Ma. She tries to decipher the secret message of the letter that her mother wrote a few weeks before Tarun arrived in Vermont. Tarun's migration was not his choice but it was thrust upon him by his own mother. The narrator has a realisation of the emotional havoc, suspended breath and the stoicism of Tarun. She becomes impatient to feel the pulse of Tarun, "I wanted to touch my fingertips to my brother's and pulse into his body all the emotions that jostled inside mine" (48). In this story Divakaruni through the matrix of familial relationship reflects on the consequences of immigration and an uncompromising longing for love in human life.

In the life of immigrants, their longing to return to their home is not only to satisfy their nostalgia but to reclaim the past and to recreate a collective history and myth of their people. The narrator of *Shame* confesses:

> What is the best thing about migrant peoples...? I think their hopefulness...and what's the worst thing? It's the emptiness of one's luggage...we've come unstruck from more than one land. We've floated upward from history, from memory, from time. (Rushdie 87)

Nostalgia for the homeland and the allurement of the hostland is the cardinal motif in the story "The Lives of Strangers". Through the antithesis of homeland and hostland, Divakaruni ventures to explore the significance of human relationship in Indian social life. The story is about the experiences of a pilgrim party from Calcutta to the holy shrine of Amarnath. Leela, an American immigrant, is also in that company. She comes to India in search of peace and religious sanctity. In the troop, Leela comes in contact of an elderly widow, Mrs. Das. She was deprived of her family and was forced to survive as a doomed widow. Leela accepts her suffering as a natural response to the American way of living. The professional and financial security in America robs people of their human ties. "In America she would have dealt with such superstition with fluent, dismissive ease, but India is complicated. Like entering a murky, primal lake, in India she has to watch her step." (58) Leela comes to India in search of spiritual peace and in her retrospection, she starts recollecting the exciting experiences of childhood like reading books, playing chess on computer and embarking on long bikes through the city.

She had left India long back to take up research projects in America where she came in contact of Mr. Dexter, another programmer. However, this relationship failed to provide her the desired physical and mental satisfaction. The uncompromising sense of loss followed by acute depression forced her to swallow sleeping pills. Ever since the failure of this relationship, she becomes impatient to go back to India in search of stable human relationship. Divakaruni explicitly exposes the filthy images of India existing in the mind of Americans or even Indians who have adopted new identities. Leela is advised by her mother, "Just be sure to take your shots before you go, drink boiled water at all times, and don't get involve in the lives of strangers" (61). The emphasis on the statement "Don't get involved in the lives of strangers" is ironical. Divakaruni argues that 'to involve' or 'not to involve' is not a matter of personal choice but is closely related with the inherent sensitivity to interpersonal relationship. Leela after her first landing at Calcutta is fascinated by cotton saries, groceries filled with odors and the morning prayers in the temple. She wears typically Bengali "Cotton Sari", looks her "raffish sauteed" with black jam and "mughlai parathas" stuffed with eggs and onions. She is thrilled by the vibrant reality of life and takes specific pleasure in unorganised ways of living. She glorifies her quest for homeland, "India was a Mardi Gras that never ended. Who would have thought she'd feel so at home here?" (63). In search of "spiritual India", she gets fascinated with the lives of strangers. She responds to the physical suffering and emotional crisis of Mrs. Das. The realisation comes to her that the bonds of human sympathy sublimates human sensibility. Through the reactions of Leela, Divakaruni exposes the crude manner of Indian life and simultaneously appreciates human values integrated in the soil of India. She confesses:

> How amazing that it should be a stranger who has opened her like a dictionary and brought to light this word whose definition has escaped her until now. (69)

In spite of physical ailments, Mrs. Das was not inclined to break her journey. After doctor's advice, like a baffled animal, she gets hold of Leela's arm and pathetically implores for her favour with such emotional bonding, Leela gets involved in the life of Mrs. Das. She admits:

> Is it pity, an emotion she has always distrusted? Is it some inchoate affinity she feels toward this stranger? But if you believe in destiny, no one can be a stranger, can they? There's always a connection, a reason because of which people enter your orbit, bristling with dark energy like a meteor intent on collision. (74)

The love and sympathy of Leela stirs a new confidence in the life of Mrs. Das. She admits that in spite of so many hurdles, at least they are "together". This idea of "togetherness" fills her with rare human sympathy. This new dimension of human sentiments makes Leela to obliterate her memories of American rearing and she seeks a fulfillment of life in the company of strangers. It was an elevation of her 'innerself' that is beyond the burden of cultural barriers and pragmatic ends. The narrator reveals this transformation of the psyche of Leela:

> Back in America, her life waits to claim her, unchanged, impervious, smelling like floor polish. In the dusty window, her reflection is a blank oval. She takes off her dark glasses to see better, but the features which peer

> back at her are unfamiliar, as though they belong to someone she has never met. (88)

Divakaruni's main occupation in this story is the celebration of humanitarian and spiritual values rooted in the soil of India. More than cultural content, her diasporic sensibility is guided by the sanctity of human relationship and it is the only realisation that generates the real sense of belongingness, rescuing the suffering humanity from being fallen in the sea of despair and despondency.

This dimension of diasporic sensibility obviously suggests that bicultural experiences are not the matter of cultural confrontation but it is a transactive aspect of colonialism in which migrant community is in persistent search of making and remaking of identities. Prof. Harish Trivedi writes:

> It may be useful to look at the whole phenomenon as a *transaction*...as an interactive, dialogic, two way process rather than a simple active-passive one: as a process involving complex negotiation and exchange. (15)

In the story "The Names of Stars in Bengali", Divakaruni in the background of mother and daughter relationship presents her defence on the problem of assimilation. The narrative is focussed on the longing for the homeland, nostalgia for the glorious past and the clash of motives in a state of cultural encounter. It is a narrative account of the experience of a lady who visits India as an American immigrant after a considerable pause of time. On her return to Calcutta, she found that her two sons were fascinated by bamboo forest, jumped up and down with a wild adrenaline and thrilled on the chanting of old rhyme. Children found it difficult to pronounce Bengali words properly. The ease of life, the innate joy and the spontaneous laughter added new dimension to their thought. It gives a new thrill of life, "Then they'd laugh again, they hadn't laughed so much in their entire lives, they'd never thought India would be this much fun, they wished they could stay for ever" (239). In spite of their pleasure, children were not able to comprehend the appropriate meaning of the stories narrated by their grandmother. In contrast of the excitement of children, she repents for being married to a foreigner. The grandmother was indifferent to the constant haunting of the past in the life of narrator. Children enjoy Indian stories, Indian foods and Indian traditions. She starts creeping into her own past. The reconstruction of past induces a greater sense of loss and nothingness. To avoid the horrors of regression, she finds it easier to assimilate in the present. When her younger son falls sick, she starts accusing the life in India. She reacts that India in spite of being a land of rich cultural heritage, can't be a safe mooring for Americans. Divakaruni notices the feeling of "guilt" and "shame" in the life of migrants. It is the guilt of violation of traditions rooted in Indian life, the guilt of allurement of the West and finally the guilt of injustice with one's own soil and self. The narrator confesses, "Oh, she should never have brought them to India, just to assuage the guilt she felt at depriving her mother of her grandchildren" (257). She reminds the incident how her mother was fainted in her longing of going back to home. Divakaruni asserts that immigration is a process of transformation from native tradition to alien traditions and the retreat in this process is not a desirable option. Assimilation is the only amicable solution of the misery born out of cultural alienation. The whole picture with vivid images has been projected in the following conclusion:

> ...But in their case, they had stepped into a time machine named immigration, and when they fell from its ferocious spinning, it was into the alien habits of a world they had imagined imperfectly. In this world, they could not inhabit a house together in the old way. They could not be mother and daughter in that way again. (261)

It indicates how insecurity, a sense of complex inability to realise the meaning of real happiness and illusion, the "glamour" of the West adversely affect the psyche of all immigrants. The irony is explicit in the life of the narrator that in spite of being a native Bengali, she cannot express herself in Bengali. Divakaruni develops the thesis that in the process of assimilation in alien culture, one loses one's own native cultural identity. She expresses her helplessness and aspires, "Maybe there's a book in there, listing the names of stars in Bengali and explaining how to identify them, which she can read to her husband and children" (268).

In this collection of short stories, the four stories "The Unknown Errors of Our Lives", "Forgotten Children", "Only the Body Knows" and "The Love of a Good Man" are the celebrations of the different dimensions of familial relationship and the subject-matter is kept apart from the issue of cross-cultural crisis.

The story "The Blooming Season for Cacti", in the background of brother and sister relationship, again highlights the issue of East-West Encounter. The narrator in the story is Mira, one sensitive Indian girl who visits her brother in California with innumerable dreams. In California, in spite of the neglect of her sister-in-law, she starts seeking the possibility of assimilation. Staying in California, her memories shift to past and present both in place and time. She recalls jostle of Bombay "torrential monsoon", "the greedy, flooded streets" and the whole ocean at night necklaced with light from marine drive. She also recalls the painful shadows of the Hindu Muslim riots. Her conscience is torn between 'home' and 'homelessness'. Her brother exhorts her: "It's not safe in India, how many times I told you and Mother this. More so now that you're unmarried and alone" (170). In this state of being unmarried and alone, she went to California where she tried to get a job at the Restaurant of Mukherjee. Though her brother was satisfied with American life and impending pride gripped his conscience. "He explained how dangerous it was, a girl traveling America alone" (175). She was appointed as a cashier and was permitted to stay in an apartment building. Priya, one of the attendents, revealed her the secret of the two marriages of Mukherjee. She inspires the narrator for marriage. She reminds her brother how there was a breach between them, "Unfortunately", she said, "time doesn't wait for women to recover. Today the men are buzzing around Mira. Tomorrow, who knows?" (183). Mira comes in contact of Radhika, Mukherjee's second wife, gets attracted by her friendship and has an insight into her miserable existence. Mira also comes in contact of Ajit, one of the regular customers at the Restaurant. His American manners fascinate her out of personal attraction, she accepts the proposal of dating with him. She could not resist her passion for his exceptional masculine personality. With Ajit she visits on Friday a particular restaurant. In these descriptions, Divakaruni makes constant references to Indian culture, tradition and Indian food habits. However in the background of Malik-Radhika relationship, Divakaruni reflects on the issue of cross-cultural marriages. Radhika tries to detain Mira because she had a realisation of the suffering of her own existence. She confesses, "I've had enough of silences. But it's not Malik I want to talk about, I learned to live with him years ago like I learnt to live with this" (196). Mira is apprehensive about the peril involved in the revelation of Radhika. Ignoring her advice, she becomes impassioned to possess the best of Ajit. Radhika fails to tolerate these advances of Mira. Divakaruni conceives that the colonial attitude initiates the annals of apathy and injustice irrespective of cultural contexts. She warns, "Not like me, Mira, I'd never want you to be like me. To make my mistakes. To end up tied to the man who tricked you in the worst way, because what else is possible in your life—" (199). In the life of Mira, the sensual passion eliminates the distinctive geographical and cultural disparities. Like a crazy girl, she starts kissing every part of Ajit's body including earlobe, throat and the curved line of collar bone. It was her attempt to rule his body. However, such an extreme and forced sexual relationship only brings a greater frustration and nothingness in her life. She accepts sex as a method of compensation for the personal loss just as she possesses a romantic longing for the beaches and deserts of California. "Sex had been a disappointment. I hadn't expected pleasure, but I had hoped for ecstasy—in the way the Greeks had meant the word. Something that you took out of yourself, made you forget who you were" (202-03). In contrast of this illusion of ecstasy, she is informed about Radhika's being in hospital, who tried to commit suicide. Malik accuses Mira for creating instability in the mind of Radhika. She becomes impatient to see Radhika and comes to a bitter realisation. "For my mother, who also believed that to save the one you love, you have to give up your own life" (208).

The in-depth analysis of the short stories collected in the volume, *The Unknown Errors of Our Lives*, provides ample evidences to establish that Divakaruni with her sensitive imagination, innate sympathy for human relationship, the awareness of perpetual binary of gender prejudices, man's innate bond of affinity with fellow beings, changed the stream of the writings of Indian diaspora. The mingling of East and West, haunting of past and present, the crisis of identity, allurement of West and the consolation of East impart a quality of richness and profoundity to the writings of Divakaruni. The perennial current of human sympathy and the longing for human love emancipate her diasporic sensibility from being localised and leads it towards the current of globalisation and universality. Her specific method of emotional affinity with an undercurrent of the sense of loss on the disintegration of human ties adds new possibilities of the perception of trauma of human existence in a state of bicultural spaces.

WORKS CITED

Divakaruni, Chitra Banerjee. *The Unknown Errors of Our Lives*. New York: Double-day—a division of Random House, Inc., 2001.

Gomez, Christina. "The On Going Quest of Bharati Mukherjee from Expatriation to Immigration." *Indian Women Novelists*, Vol. 5, ed. R.K. Dhawan. Delhi: Prestige Publication, 1995.

Jain, Jasbir. "Introduction." *Writers of Indian Diaspora*. Jaipur: Rawat Publication. 2003.

——. "Geographical Dislocation and the Poetics of Exile: Ashis Gupta and Michael Ondaatje." *Writers of Indian Diaspora*. Jaipur: Rawat Publication, 2003.

Lopez, Berry. "A Literature of Place." *A Sense of Place: Regional American Literature*. Delhi: USIS, August 1976.

Mukherjee, Bharati. "A Wife's Story." *Middleman and Other Stories*. New Delhi: Prentice Hall of India, 1989.

Rushdie, Salman. *Shame*. New Delhi: Rupa & Co., 1983.

Trivedi, Harish. *Colonial Transactions: English Literature and India*. Calcutta: Papyrus.

Chitra Banerjee Divakaruni's *Arranged Marriage*: A Perspective

17

Shalini Gupta

Chitra Divakaruni is America based writer of Indian origin whose work is partially autobiographical. Not only are most of her stories set in the Bay Area of California, but she also deals with the immigrant experience. Since 1991, she has been the President of Maitri, a helpline for South Asian women that particularly helps victims of domestic violence and other abusive situation. She says that she sees herself as "a listener, a facilitator, a connector to people," and, "to me, the art of dissolving boundaries is what living is all about". No wonder, much of Divakaruni's writing centers around the lives of immigrant women, as she candidly admits:

> Women in particular respond to my work because I'm writing about them, women in love, in difficulties, women in relationships. I want people to relate to my characters, to feel their joy and pain, because it will be harder to [be] prejudiced when they meet them in real life. (Softky)

Chitra's poems and stories focus on the experiences and struggles of women trying to find their own identities:

> India—born girls and women who are torn between two cultures receive a fine collection of stories which examine women's independence and roles under India's social constraints. These are excellent, hard-hitting stories which are revealing and engrossing. (Midwest Book Review)

Arranged Marriage received considerable critical acclaim and the 1996 American Book Award, The Bay Area Book Reviews and PEN Oakland Awards for fiction. In *Arranged Marriage,*

Divakaruni encompasses a wide variety of themes including racism, interracial relationships, economic disparity, abortion, and divorce. She "was really consumed by these stories and the need to write them" (Neela Banerjee).

As stated in her numerous interviews and non-fictional writings, Chitra Divakaruni focuses her critical lenses on arranged marriages of Indian women living in India and India born women living new lives in America. Specially, the women in India are subjected to ghoulish, brutish and nasty treatment in married lives that they become a martyr as a result of their ages-old servitude. The hoary tradition of finding matches by matching the horoscopes of the boy and the girl sometimes miserably fails to assure domestic bliss to the beleaguered women, instead the domestic violence predominates. "The Bats" is the opening story of *Arranged Marriage* which portrays the pitiable plight of a woman who becomes a prisoner in an arranged marriage. The domestic violence is unleashed upon her each night. It seems she has formed an interminable alliance with sobs, sighs and tears. Ma bears with the subhuman existence as she has no one to go back to except an old uncle in the countryside.

The Ma in the story is like overwhelming number of mothers in many homes in India who are subjected to worst forms of physical abuse that they begin to form an alliance with grief throughout their uneventful lives. One night Ma stealthily slips away, along with her daughter, from the cruel clutches of her husband, to an uncle living in a remote village. Some time passes gleefully for the mother and the daughter but "the stares and whispers of the women in the marketplace" and the "loneliness of being without him [husband]" (12) proves too much for her and she fires off a letter to her husband. The husband writes back and promises "it won't happen again" (11) and she readies herself to join him. But after return the physical assaults on her person do not stop, each night leaves its own scars on her face, she escapes again from the barbarities of the marriage but like a dog who returns to his own vomit, the Ma too returns to the prison-house of marriage which provides her neither any relief nor any sense of respectability.

Affair is an interesting story involving two couples—Ashok and Abha and Meena and Srikant. Like other stories in the collection, this story too throws up the existential dilemmas of the immigrant Indians who carry the baggage of Indian cultural values, which in the changed scenario of freedom and choices, becomes anachronistic. The two couples are leading a transparently peaceful life but beneath the surface there seems to be a simmering discontent which never gets articulated either in words or in actions. The revelation of Meena having an affair becomes the flash point in the life of Abha who begins to evaluate herself and the insipid marriage in which she feels trapped and "still suffering from [her] prudish Indian upbringing" (234). These two childless but young couples prima facie lead a tranquil life but gradually the coolness creeps invisibly into their relationships. Meena regards her husband Srikant's obsession with his work and computer beyond tolerance as "Srikant would stay on at work till all kinds of hours, even though I kept telling him I hated being alone in the house. It was so deathly quiet..." (239). She, unlike her friend Abha, looked for excitement, novelty and charm in married life. Abha's husband Ashok too expects forbidden thrills in marriage which she regards as obnoxious and antithetical to the values that have been ingrained in her. Essentially Meena and Ashok complement each other, while Abha and Srikant have certain defined common frequencies. Meena's search for her Animus ends in finding an American lover but it triggers off a process of self-introspection in Abha who "has begun to pull the unraveled edges of [her] existence into a new design" (272). What colours Srikant or Suren Gupta would bring to the envisioned design of Abha, is left for the readers to speculate. One thing, however, is absolutely clear that like Meena, Abha too has cleared the gates of her vision, and is all set to have it out with her husband, Ashok. A voice inside Abha intones: "It's better this way, each of us freeing the other before it's too late...so we can start learning, once more, to live" (271-72).

Debjani Banerjee contends that the tradition of arranged marriages that ostensibly underpins Indian culture, implicates individuals in gender hierarchies and naturalizes these inequities through stereotypes of masculinity and feminity. Deemed as superior to other kinds of marriages where the individuals assert their choice, the institution is notorious for its commodification of women, specially in the context of bride-viewing sessions that unmarried girls are subjected to. The relationship between Abha and Meena in *Affair*, builds the space of intervention that enables both women to extricate themselves from meaningless relationships and re-write their strategies of survival. As in Divakaruni's stories, the women frequently leave their marriages or relationships in order to re-conceptualize their notions of self and home.

The Disappearance is another story in the anthology which explores the cross-cultural experiences of a woman through a feminist perspective. The writer has sensitively portrayed the extent of the woman's oppression within the marriage in which the wife is not allowed to pursue her financial independence, rather she is subject to marital rape. The husband is completely confounded when his wife 'disappears' as for him his wife is a symbol of his financial and sexual power. Carrying the patriarchal baggage the husband cannot even begin to understand individual desire for some space and autonomy. After his wife's disappearance, the husband reflects on his conjugal life.

The Indian male's cultural obsessions vis-a-vis the wife, are revealed through his reflections:

> He was a good husband. No one could deny it. He let her have her way, indulged her, even.... Once in a while, of course, he had to put his foot down, like when she wanted to get a job or go back to school or buy American clothes. But he always softened his no's with a remark like, What for, I'm here to take care of you.... He would pull her onto his lap and give her a kiss and a cuddle which usually ended with him taking her to the bedroom.... That was another area where he'd had to be firm. Sex. She was always saying, Please not tonight, I don't feel up to it. (171-72)

In a veiled manner Divakaruni asserts that in arranged marriages, attempts to schedule an expression of female sexuality to coincide with institutional structures of marriage renders impossible an articulation of women's desires. At the end of the story, the wife leaves with her jewellery to set up her own economic unit within which she can reformulate her own identity.

Although the situations and characters vary, the themes of the short stories in *Arranged Marriage* are essentially the same exploration of the nature of arranged marriages as well as the experience of affirmation and rebellion against social traditions. Divakaruni beautifully tells stories about immigrant brides who are "both liberated and trapped by cultural changes" and who are struggling "to carve out an identity of their own" (San Francisco Chronicle). *Doors* epitomizes the conjugal clash between Deepak and Preeti as that of confrontation between two cultures. Preeti loves the Western idea of privacy. Their domestic peace is shattered when Deepak's friend Raj from India arrives to live with them, the new arrival intrudes into the space commonly shared by the husband and the wife. Deepak's traditional self emerges strongly much to the chagrin of his wife and he begins to enlighten his wife about the virtues of the traditional Indian wife "to be obedient and adjusting and forgiving" (184). Preeti yearns for moments of privacy and some space in her own home, "Even family members sometimes need time and space away from each other. In my family no one ever intruded" (198). Reeling under the unbearable weight of encroachment upon her sense of privacy and space she thinks "This can't be happening to me," (196) because "All her life she had believed that she could do anything she set her mind to; it was what her mother had always said. Now as a sudden wave of giddiness struck her, she felt doubt for the first time. I won't let him ruin my life, she said. For a moment it wasn't clear to her if it was Raj she was referring to, or Deepak" (197). Toward the conclusion of the story there is little doubt that the *door* which symbolized space and privacy for Preeti, finally "clicked shut deep inside her own being" (202).

Meeting Mrinal is another manifestation of how marriages, arranged or otherwise go sour when the anticipations of the partner/s in a marriage do not fructify. Mahesh divorces Asha after more than ten years of marriage, to live with Jessica and Asha is left to fend for herself and take care of the growing teen-aged son, Dinesh who like most of the America born children of Indian immigrants adopts the ways, manners and jargon which exasperate his mother, born and bred on a rich diet of Indian cultural values. Asha too, like the Ma in the story, "The Bats", cannot tolerate the jibes and taunts of the wagging tongues of the women at the social gatherings, about her divorced status:

> But I'd be the only woman in the room without a husband, and the other wives, even those too well bred to whisper, would look at me with pity, as though at something maimed, an animal with a limb chopped off. Behind the pity would be a flicker of gratitude that it hadn't happened to them, or a gleam of suspicion because now I was unattached and therefore dangerous. (277)

It is neither Asha's extramarital affair or any adulterous act that drives Mahesh away from her. It is rather the realization that all along he has lived life according to the exigencies of time and situation, and a situation had arrived in his life when he resolves to loosen himself from the straitjackets that he had been forced by the circumstances to wear as a son, husband and father. After having lived for others, Dinesh decides to live life on his own independent terms:

> All his life, he told [Asha] then, he'd been doing what other people wanted, being a dutiful son, then a responsible husband and father. Now he'd finally found someone who made him feel alive, happy. He wanted the chance to really live his life before it was too late. (286-87)

When life depressed Asha with its clutter and its ordinariness, she thinks of her friend Mrinal who she thinks "has the perfect existence—money, freedom, admiration" (288) in being unmarried. Both of them had been brought up by mothers who believed that "women should be happy with whatever their men decided they ought to have. A woman who grasped things for herself, we had heard over and over, was greedy. Selfish" (292).

Mrinal's economic independence fails to fill the vacuum in her life yet she is conscious:

> There's a lot in my life that I'm proud of. The freedom. The power. Walking into a room full of men knowing none of them can push me around. Seeing the reluctant admiration in their eyes when I close a tough deal...I'd never give it up to dwindle into a wife, like that woman. (294)

Deep down in her heart Mrinal is conscious of what she has lost in the process as she advises Asha to adore the two men in her life, husband Mahesh and son, Dinesh, then she grounds her knuckles into her eyes and weeps her heart out. At this point of time Asha has a revelation that "perfection was only a mirage".

Her stories have prompted some to accuse Divakaruni of tarnishing the Indian community's image and reinforcing stereotypes of the "oppressed" Indian women, but as Julie Mehta tells us, the writer herself claimed that her aim was to shatter stereotypes:

> Some just write about different things, but my approach is to tackle these sensitive topics. I hope people who read my book will not think of the characters as Indians, but feel for them as people.

Chitra Divakaruni writes about what she feels strongly about and one of these is the complicated position of Indian women and their challenges. She writes about many positive things too, about strong family bonds and the courage of people who find themselves in a different world after immigration. In short, we can say that she portrays Indians in a balanced light. Chitra Divakaruni, like other Diasporic women writers, articulates in her books "the deepest fear and trauma faced by women in India and here [U.S.A.]—and show them emerge, at least, in many cases, as stronger and self-reliant women" (Kamath). Let us not be judgmental about the portrayal of a battered wife, a single mother, a divorced woman, a westernized Indian woman or ruptured human relationships in arranged marriages or otherwise. The dynamics of life conjure up certain truths which constrain one to concur with Divakaruni that in an arranged marriage or otherwise "No one has a perfect life. Perhaps our mistake is in thinking we need to have perfect lives" (Mehta). This is what dawns upon Asha in *Meeting Mrinal,* as she legitimately, albeit painfully, discovers that "perfection was only a mirage" (296).

WORKS CITED

Banerjee, Debjani "Home and Us: Redefining Identity in the South Asian Diaspora through the Writings of Chitra Banerjee Divakaruni and Meena Alexander." *The Diasporic Imagination: Asian-American Writing.* Ed. Somdatta Mandal. New Delhi: Prestige, 2000.

Banerjee, Neela. "Mistress of Self" @www.asianweek.com

Divakaruni, Chitra Banerjee. *Arranged Marriage.* London: 1995, rpt. Black Swan Book, 1997. (All references incorporated in the text are from this edition.)

Kamath, A.P. "Women Writers of Indian Diaspora Create a Big Impact." Rediff on the net, August 23, 1999.

Mehta, Julie. "Sunnyvale Author Chitra Divakaruni Talks About Marriages and Stereotypes." @ www. metro, May 8-14, 1997.

Softky, Elizabeth. "A Cross-cultural Understanding Spiced with the Indian Diaspora." @Black Issue.

Kiran Desai's *The Inheritance of Loss*: An Expression of Hypocrisy

18

Satendra Kumar and *Manoj Kumar*

Newcomer Kiran Desai, who is currently a student in Columbia University's creative writing course, was born in India in 1971 and educated in India, England and the United States. She is the daughter of universally acclaimed Indian novelist, Anita Desai. Kiran Desai was fifteen when she left India—she lived in England for a year and has been in the US since then—and it's tempting to pigeonhole her as another NRI writer obsessed by the themes like dislocation (something that certainly runs through *Inheritance)*. In person, however, she comes across as someone who's never really felt out of place, no matter where she's been. She's pleasingly not conscious about the topic of immigrants, joking (again from the outside, as if she isn't personally involved) about the various kinds there are: "those who throw up their hands at the difficulties—and, at the other end of the scale, those who are expert at playing the ethnic card, accentuating the character traits they are expected to have, and thereby making a success of their lives" (www.Amazon.com). Desai feels 'no alienation or dislocation'.

Kiran Deasi has written two novels *Hullabaloo under the Guava Orchard* and *The Inheritance of Loss*. The present article is a modest attempt to decipher at hatching the graph of the lives of hypocrisy through the character of Gyan, so called Mathematics tutor. Kiran Desai reveals in one of the interviews, "I think there are several kinds of loss that happen in this book. It is really a book about characters that have been forced to live half-lives or lives of hypocrisy because of the circumstances that they find themselves in. I found that when I was writing it, everyone had that half-story to tell, which together added up to a picture that I felt was whole" (Interview). In the same interview, Desai herself unlocks, "I have really tried to capture the patterns—the emotional and historical patterns that I have witnessed. It has been a history that is caught between East and West and traveling back and forth." In the words of Roxana Robinson as marked on the cover page, "A whirlwind of a novel, rich and sad and funny. Kiran Desai moves between New York and the northeast corner of India; between the sense of loss and the sense of possession; between the big notion of colonialism and the small notion of intimacy. Desai's enchanting—often hilarious—descriptions are a pleasure to read."

This majestic novel of a busy, grasping time—every moment holding out the possibility of hope or betrayal—opens with the following lines:

> *All day*, the colors had been those of dusk, mist moving like a water creature across the great flanks of mountains possessed of ocean shadows and depths. Briefly visible above the vapor, Kanchenjunga was a far peak whittled out of ice, gathering the last of the light, a plume of snow blown high by the storms at its summit.
>
> Sai, sitting on the veranda, was reading an article about giant squid in an old *National Geographic*. (The Inheritance of Loss 1)

Set in the mid-1980s in Kalimpong, high in the northeastern Himalayas, *The Inheritance of Loss* centers on three people and one dog living together in an ancient house named Cho Oyu. There's the embittered, reptilian judge, lost in his chessboard and in his memories: of a youth spent at Cambridge many decades earlier; of humiliation in a foreign land. Staying with him (in this order of affection received) are his beloved dog Mutt and his 17-year-old granddaughter Sai, who was orphaned as a child. The judge's cook, who manages the household, and a few neighbours scattered around the area, round off the cast. As the story unfolds, insurgency is growing in the region: the Indian Nepalese want their own country or state, a Gorkhaland where they will not be treated as servants; young boys trying to be men, roam the mountainside looting houses, collecting ammunition. Their predicament is contrasted against that of Indians settled abroad (the cook's son Biju, stumbling from one job to the next in the US, in a humorous parallel narrative).

Sai, who was studying in St. Augustine's Convent, heard the news of the death of her parents who were crashed by the local bus wheels, that orphaned her and compelled her to take haven in the house of retired Judge, residing in isolated house at the foot of Mount Kanchenjunga in Himalayas. Judge was served by a faithful cook who was always lost in memory of his lovable son Biju, illegal immigrant in New York for job. The Judge first appointed Nonita or Noni as a tutor to teach Sai—science to Shakespeare. It was only when Noni's abilities in Maths and Science began to falter when Sai was sixteen that the Judge was forced to hire Gyan, twenty years old pal to take over these subjects.

It was Feb 1986, Sai was seventeen and her romance with Gyan, the mathematics tutor, was not even a year old:

> Could fulfillment ever be felt as deeply as loss? Romantically she decided that love must surely reside in the gap between desire and fulfillment, in the lack, not the contentment. Love was the ache, the anticipation, the retreat, everything around it but the emotion itself. (2-3)

When Gyan came to teach Sai, the very first day his eyes rested directly upon her as if he were eating her alive in an orgy of the imagination. That night Sai sat and stared into the mirror:

> Sitting across from Gyan, she had felt so acutely aware of herself, she was certain it was because of his gaze on her, but every time she glanced up, he was looking in another direction. (74)

Over the days, she found herself continually obsessed with her own face, aware that she was meanwhile whiting her aptitude for something else. When Sai became interested in love, she became interested in other people's love affairs, and she pestered the cook about the judge and his wife.

The novelist depicted the lives of their hypocrisy step by step in the novel in an exotic manner as if the novelist might have experienced in her life. In the drawing room sitting with newspapers, Sai and Gyan were left alone, quite alone, for the first time. Their eyes read on industriously, but their thoughts didn't cleave to such discipline, and finally Gyan, unable to bear this any longer, this tightrope tension between them, put down his paper with a crashing sound, turned abruptly toward her, and blurted:

> "Do you put oil in your hair?"
>
> "No," she said, startled. "I never do."
>
> After a bit of silence, "Why?" she asked. "Was there something wrong with her hair?"
>
> "I can't hear you—the rain is so loud," he said, moving closer.
>
> "What?"
>
> "Why?"
>
> "It looks so shiny I thought you might."
>
> "No."
>
> "It looks very soft," he observed. "Do you wash it with shampoo?"
>
> "Yes."
>
> "What kind?"
>
> "Sunsilk."
>
> Oh, the unbearable intimacy of brand names, the boldness of the questions.
>
> "What soap?"
>
> "Lux."
>
> "Beauty bar of the film stars?"
>
> "Let me see your hands. They are so small."
>
> "Are they?"
>
> "Yes." He held his own out by hers. "See?"
>
> Fingers, nails.
>
> "*Hm.* What long fingers. Little nails. But look, you bite them."

He weighed her hand.

"Light as a sparrow. The bones must be hollow". (114-15)

So they played the game of courtship, reading, retreating, teasing, molesting, intoxicating and fleeing. "Kiss me!" He pleaded. "No," she said, delighted and terrified. Moments clocked by precisely, and finally she couldn't bear it—she closed her eyes and felt the terrified measure of his lips on hers, trying to match one shape with the other. And there was a flood of kisses one after another without a moment's delay:

"Nose?" He kissed it.

"Eyes?" Eyes.

"Ears?" Ears.

"Cheek?" Cheek.

"Fingers." one, two, three, four, five.

"The other hand, please." Ten kisses.

"Toes?" (125)

Thus Gyan and Sai's romance was flourishing. The novelist captured the moment in the novel.

The character of Gyan is depicted by the novelist like the butterfly tasting and sipping the pollen from different flowers and resting no where. In one of the scenes Gyan was found by Sai red handed in voluptuous critical situation: "Does Gyan live here?" Sai asked despite herself. Suspicion shadowed the girl's face. It was an old, unsurprised sureness of ulterior motives, a funny look in a child. "He's my mathematics tutor," answered the other girl. Still looking as if someone like Sai could only mean trouble, she set down the pot and went back into the house as the rooster rushed forth to peck the grain stuck at the bottom, climbing right inside, giving the hens a reprieve. At that moment, Gyan came out, caught her expression of distaste before she had a chance to disguise it, and was outraged. Gyan said, "How dare she seek him out to find her indulgence in pity!" He had been feeling guilty about his extended silence, was considering of returning to see her, but now he knew he was quite right. The rooster climbed out of the pot and began to strut about. He was the only grand thing around, crowned, spurred, crowing like a colonial: "What do you want?" asked Gyan. She saw his thoughts recast his eyes and mouth, remembered that he had abandoned her, not the other way around, and she was bitterly angry:

> Dirty hypocrite.
>
> Pretending one thing, living another. Nothing but lies through and through. (256-57)

Above everything else, though *The Inheritance of Loss* is a tender meditation on loving and loss, it is about how, in all our different ways, we wish to fit in. The fact of exile and how that exile affects the notion of home, how it colors perception and how it heightens the sense of wanting to belong are strong currents that run through this novel and make it a parable of times. In a generous vision, sometimes funny, sometimes sad, Desai presents the human quandaries facing a panoply of characters. Kirshenbaum, the author of *An Almost Perfect Moment* unearths:

> A nation's tragedies, great and small are revealed through the hopes and the dreams, the innocence and the assonance, the love betrayed and the all—too human failings of a superbly realized cast of characters. (Qtd. On cover page)

Whatever be the love and deportment of Gyan to Sai but Sai thought with a burst of hope. A message: 'I will love you after all' and the novel sums up happily:

> The five peaks of Kanchenjunga turned golden with the kind of luminous light that made you feel, if briefly, that truth was apparent. All you needed to do was to reach out and pluck it. (324)

WORKS CITED

Desai, Kiran. *The Inheritance of Loss*. New Delhi: Penguin Books India Pvt. Ltd., 2006.

——. "Interview." *The Sunday Hindustan Times*, 22 January 2006.

http://www.Amazon.Com/Books: *The Inheritance of Loss*.

Quest for Identity in Iqbal Ramoowalia's *The Death of a Passport*

19

T.S. Anand

Diaspora is a term used by historians to refer to those settlements inhabited by Jews in all parts of the world outside the state of Israel. The Diaspora, as the term is now used, has come to mean any sizable community of a particular nation living outside its own country and sharing some common bonds that give them any ethnic identity and consequent bonding. Today there are over twenty million people of Indian origin spread across a hundred and ten countries. These people, originally hailing from the Third World countries and now free in the First World, were not forcibly moved from their locations. Dislocation was a matter of choice, and exile is not necessarily something which ought to generate angst, though we do see in some writers evidence of angst.

Diaspora literature produced by diasporic writers of such diversity as V.S. Naipaul, Salman Rushdie, Bharati Mukherjee, Rohinton Mistry, Chitra Divakaruni, Meena Alexander, Jhumpa Lahiri, Iqbal Ramoowalia and many others, explores problems and possibilities engendered by the experience of migrancy and diaspora life. In the process of engaging and negotiating notions of history, identity, gender, cultural and racial purity, the works of these writers graphically portray their ethnic, cultural and religious situatedness. Iqbal Ramoowalia, Indian-Canadian novelist, offered the following comments on the Diasporic literature and the issues that constantly mirror up in such writings:

> Diasporic literature reflects challenges, aspirations, and anxieties of a person who migrates to a new land. The first generation of all immigrants always suffers from a

> broad sense of nostalgia, and the first generation immigrants tend to cling strenuously together in order to preserve their cultural, religious and linguistic identity. Preserving their identity is one of their chief concerns.[1]

The present paper focuses upon Iqbal Ramoowalia's maiden novel *The Death of a Passport.* Like many other Diasporic writings, the novel portrays quite sensitively the precarious predicament and angst of the illegals in Canada who do not want to be caught and deported but "sniff around for ways to secure salvation from uncertainty". Their assumption of new identities to circumvent the immigration laws, is one of the survival strategies. The protagonist Seema Malhotra is one of the myriad instances of parents' undiminished craze to marry their daughters to the immigrants from Canada, America, UK etc. After marriage with Anmol, Seema reaches Canada on a tourist visa, the marriage falls apart, and she is deprived of the custody of her infant son and the immigrant status. She reaches Toronto to face rigours and travails of illegal stay.

The Death of a Passport (2004) chronicles the immigrant angst and quest for identity of Seema, an illegal immigrant in Canada who meanders through the Metropolitan jungle of Toronto, infested with male marauders whose lustful obnoxious behaviour scars Seema psychologically and fiscally. The author, a prominent Punjabi poet immigrated to Canada in the mid-1970s, and like any new immigrant, earned a wealth of experience through odd jobs as laborer, a dishwasher, a security guard and a taxi driver. His protracted encounters with the bitter and brutish realities that obtain in the "Promised Land" of milk and honey, and his exposure to the academic milicu of Waterloo, Dalhousie and York universities left an indelible imprint on his mental make-up. No doubt, Iqbal Ramoowalia "suffered a lot of racism and discrimination" in the multicultural milieu of Canada but these encounters, as he explained to me through an e-mail, have rendered him "more tolerant and more broadminded." There is no visible bitterness or rancour in his portrayal of the series of agonies, physical abuse, financial exploitation and mental torture experienced by Seema. The novelist alludes to the stark naked reality which robs an individual of the last vestige of humanity, respectability and identity in an alien milieu:

> Alien places pose innumerable challenges for survival, and being illegal makes one doubly vulnerable. That's a universal truth. Seema symbolizes immigrants of all shapes and hues: They, like Seema invariably suffer mentally, physically, emotionally and financially. Seema rolls from one place to another and from one person to another and in this process, she looses her name, her aspiration and her family...Fear and loss of identity... constantly torment new immigrants.

As the narrative unfolds, it is "chilling January night in Vancouver" as Seema sits by her infant son Amroz, and feels herself "like an ant...an unwanted presence in that lavishly furnished elephantine house." The reader discerns the wide chasm that exists between Seema and her husband Anmol as the numerous questions concerning her predicament raise their heads like a hooded cobra:

> Why do I wait for Anmol every single night in spite of this invisible fog thickly stretched between us? Why? What is left between us to continue living together in this elegant house? Who are we to each other? (*The Death of a Passport,* 5)

Yet Seema like the narrator is conscious of the ancient servility that is a legacy of the Indian woman: "The age-old Indian woman's obedience...coaxing her to replay the centuries old ritual of standing up speechless, hands assuming a folded posture...in the fashion of bond maids of legendary palaces of the Maharajas...Indian husbands are unquestionably Maharajas." Seema feels irked by what legends and parables accentuate that "the wife has to be a faithful attendant, tongueless and blind" (7). The discomforting phase in Seema's married life caused by her confession of a man in her pre-marital phase of life, had resulted in the conspicuous strangulation of speech and the decision to separate. The anticipated arrival of Anmol's mother from India was a signal to Seema to quickly pack off her paltry paraphernalia, to call her friend Veena in Toronto to pick her up at Toronto airport, a covert cue to call a taxicab to get to Vancouver Airport. At this critical juncture Seema's six month-old-son was her crucifying concern.

The ephemeral marriage to Anmol had transformed Seema Malhotra into Seema Malik, it had also plunged her into a life of uncertainty marked by a constant fear of being caught and deported to India. She imagines herself to be a tiny Buddha with her trivial quest for fulfillment:

> We all are tiny Buddhas with our trivial quests for fulfillment of our frivolous desires. The proportions of salvation we seek in our perfect correspondence with the sizes of the Buddhas our trivial selves grow into. (50)

In order to conceal her illegal status Seema is compelled to wrap different personas around herself, and philosophizes: "Hiding is what this world is much about.... Hiding is a feeling and being secure" (52). However, the sense of security is very fragile as without much coveted landed stamp or Social Insurance Number, the illegals have to sweat out for longer hours but lesser wages. Thus begins the process of exploitation which is further compounded if the victim happens to be a hapless woman, an easy bait for prowlers, confidence tricksters, and thugs pretending to be saviors.

Out of Veena's house where Ajeet, her husband had nearly raped Seema, she becomes a rudderless boat which finds a sojourn with, Rajan Brar who helps in assuming a new identity as Reeta Gill whose Social Insurance Number she uses to earn her livelihood by hoodwinking the law. Seema, as Reeta Gill, through her loyalty and perseverance, demonstrates her resilient spirit and wins the trust of her benefactor and employer. All along she was tormented at being divested of an integral part of her being, and felt like, "crying at the loss of something inseparable from her" because her public posturing as Reeta Gill meant wearing "somebody else cast off clothes"(83). The nagging feeling of being deprived of her true identity: "Who am I?...hiding from myself yet in the deepest recesses of her heart Seema wanted "to be Seema"(95). Her deep desire and wish to be Seema has to be weighed against the necessity of being Reeta Gill yet the longing to be Seema persists.

The angst of an illegal immigrant finds no better illustration than Seema's abandoning of her assumed identity as Reeta Gill. Her desperation to be free from uncertainty takes her to Patricia's restaurant whose compassion gets better of her thinking faculty. She employs Seema, and rechristens her as Susan Shaw. At Patricia's restaurant Seema meets Sodhi, an agent of her salvation who files papers for marriage with Seema, as her marriage to an authentic immigrant could alone lend legality to her stay in Canada. Sodhi, orphaned at seven, had his tryst with the criminal world, amassed money through cheating, smuggling opium and pimping and mastered the art to hoodwink the insurance companies through false and exaggerated claims. Living in Sodhi's house in a new *avatar* Seema's *mantra* was to "please the devil...and get *nirvana* from the ferocious jaws of the law-enforcing hawks" (200). As Seema Sodhi she would let him unleash his slime into her passive body every night because through him throbbed Seema's hope "to achieve salvation from her tortuous state of uncertainty" (203). What Seema longs for does not happen, and what happens so suddenly she did not anticipate. At this point of time "cursed sighs and sobs formed an eternal bond with Seema" (238). Her quest for salvation and a legal residence gets halted traumatically with Sodhi's tragic untimely death. Thus, her journey from Seema Malhotra—to Seema Malik—to Reeta Gill—to Susan Shaw—to Seema Sodhi halts abruptly, and the novelist successfully emphasizes that "immigrants' struggle never ends as life itself is open ended." Toward the conclusion of the novel Seema is all set for "an another blind flight without wings in quest of another passport with a landed stamp before the cruel noose of immigration closed around her neck for a quick deportation." Seema may be exhausted a bit in her interminable quest for identity yet the narrative reveals her bracing up for quest to know "Who am I?"

NOTE

1. T.S. Anand, spoke recently with Iqbal Ramoowalia via e-mail about his first novel, the definition of Diasporic Literature and the universal dimensions of his work.

WORKS CITED

Braziel, Jana Evans and Anita Mannur. Eds. *Theorizing Diaspora: A Reader*. Oxford: U.K. Blackwell, 2003.

Kaur, Tejinder and N.K. Neb. Eds. *Perspectives on Diaspora: Indian Fiction in English*. Jalandhar: Nirman Publication, 2005.

Ramoowalia, Iqbal. *The Death of a Passport*. Delhi: Ajanta Book International, 2004.

Human Bonds and Vikram Seth

20

Malti Sharma

The whole world has been defined afresh and so also has literature been. Vikram Seth is quite befitting to supply the intellectual demands of this widening world. In this global village, no writer can be satisfied just by catering to needs of a country or so. They are bound to deal with the essential material, which is known as global and universal. Outward picture can be different but the essence everywhere is the same. On humanitarian grounds, what troubles the most powerful nation or individual, is exactly the worry of the weakest too. T.S. Eliot, the renowned Western critic, in 'The Waste Land', has aptly expressed this idea when he calls man 'fear in a handful of dust'. He confirms that it is fear and insecurity that surrounds man in West or East. This provides us with a clue to understand the inner world of man. No Indian or American material, but a true literary genius—Vikram Seth writes at a plane which is above geographical or historical boundaries. Starting with poetry, he found himself writing huge novels, manifesting grand narrative skill, not only in poetry but in poetic fiction also. Human bonds, as strong as rope of steel and as soft as a sigh, have been the material that Vikram Seth has used to give us an engaging and exciting picture of outer, as well as, inner situations of human life.

Enriching the world of Indian English literature in quantity and quality both, making news for the huge sum advanced to him for his recent work *Two Lives*, Vikram Seth is known as no lesser than a literary giant. Style-wise he is a mastermind as a novel *The Golden Gate*, stretching in over 600 old sonnets, is not an ordinary creation. As it is, sporting with words comes out of his powerful command over language. All this apart, his fictional world is covered by a network of relationships and bonds, which, for him, seem to have universal value. It is not for nothing that he has been called forever a child of his extended family. Vikram Seth offers an enchanting world of living men and women in his works, alive—not as in flesh and blood, but very much in their relationship with each other. Their love is constant and unconditional, if not vigorous, their hatred is given a space, if not cancelled. In an interview to Tim Adams for 'The Hindu' he admits "My family has been the biggest thing in my life." He knows very well that, every relationship offers you, some amount of assurance followed by fears. He cherishes the assurance, as passionately as he accepts the fears. His writing and real life are so well intertwined, that almost each of his characters is a tribute to each of his cherished relationship in life.

His latest work *Two Lives* sets the clock back to give us a breath-taking account of India, the Third Reich and the Second World War, Auschwitz and the Holocaust, Israel and Palestine, Post war Germany and 1970s Britain. Seth himself says: 'It has a complex graph of love' in various relationships. *A Suitable Boy* is woven around, almost all the real-life bonds, lived intensely on the planes of reality. It begins with ridiculing the celebration of marriage but ends with a cool-headed decision, in favour of bonds through marriage. *The Golden Gate* is a novel in verse, which gives us a bored and frustrated generation (represented by John), who finds that nothing holds him. He tries relationships but in a mechanical fashion and, no wonder, he fails and is "caught in the kelp of loneliness, he cries for help" (4). *Equal Music* shows love and music playing on the emotions and reiterates Seth's philosophy of the value of such mundane institutions as home and family, which are seen as cradle of bonds. It explores the loneliness of an artist and role of his bonding with music. To sum up, bonds, deep and strong, are a peculiar feature of the material Vikram Seth uses in his works. His social concern peeps through his respect for bonds. It is not a justification of bonds just because he has got into them, but the bonds that he got naturally through birth, or chose through friendship—are so important for him that he says: 'my family is my religion' (Interview with Tim Adams).

Starting his career with *Mappings* (1980), an introspective work, abounding in themes of love, friendship, loneliness, loss, expatriation, nature, and others—Seth moved on to a series of poetic compositions namely *From Heaven Lake* (a travelogue published in 1983) and *The Humble Administrator's Garden* (1985). Then appeared *The Golden Gate* in 1986—a grand display of poetic narration which won him Commonwealth Poetry Prize for the year and Seth, spontaneously, was shot into limelight. This novel claimed another award (the Central Sahitya Academy Award) in 1988. Three more volumes of poetry followed—*All You Who Sleep Tonight* (1990) *Beastly Tales from Here and There* (1991) and *Three Chinese Poets* (1993). *All You Who Sleep Tonight* is intensely personal, dealing with love, friendship, familial ties and the loneliness of living in a foreign land. Glamour of western world is not powerful enough to replace his nears and dears. *Beastly Tales from Here and There* is a delightful collection of fables retold in verse with Seth's inimitable charm. The themes are essentially social and humanitarian. Seth gives them a subtle twist, to make the stories co-temporal in their relevance to the ironies of life. *Three Chinese Poets* is the final product of Seth's stay in China, reflecting on Seth's interest in literature as an art.

A Suitable Boy (1993) gave the author a chance to create literary history not only with the book's mammoth size but also with a record sale of million copies. Though the subject matter of *A Suitable Boy* is India of 1950's, yet it cannot be taken strictly as an Indian novel as the author is not seen forcing his ethnicity on the reader. This was followed by an opera *Arion and the Dolphin* (1994), based on the classical story of the musician Arian. *An Equal Music* (1999), an extraordinary novel about music and love, came as a result of something that was since long, struggling inside the fertile mind of Seth. Ever since his childhood he had learnt to play flute and was trained to sing. Later, at Oxford, he was introduced to Western classical music. This turned into a life-long passion for music. Coupled with deep sensibility of a writer, it attained ultimate meanings in *An Equal Music.* After a gap of six years came, *Two Lives* (2005) that proved to be yet another landmark in Seth's career on account of the novel's unprecedented welcome. Evidently, Seth's writings spontaneously serve as a window to display the new generation's point of view. But at the same time senior generations or their values are not unseated in his literature. He has rather nourished and glorified them throughout his works. In addition to this, he provides a platform for debating on the relevance of new and the old. Human relationship and bonds is one area which Vikram Seth wouldn't change for anything. There is an intricate thread-work of relationships and human bonds which has been used to weave the canvas of his literary portrayals.

His first novel *The Golden Gate* has been hailed as the great Californian novel because of the themes it treats; disillusionment from love, estrangement, discontent at the work-place, Silicon valley, nuclear bombs, one-night-stands, homosexuality, rock-music—all that present the reality of an American dream. Walking across 'Golden Gate Park' is a bored, frustrated and depressed generation represented by John. He tries relationships in a mechanical fashion, drops them, and finally suffers their absence. Seth highlights fears of this rootless and fruitless mind:

> Successful in his field, though only
> Twenty Six, respected, lonely
> One evening as he walked across
> Golden Gate Park, the ill judged toss
> Of red frisbee almost brained him
> He thought, "If I died, who'd be sad?
> Who'd weep, who'd gloat, who'd be glad?
> Would anybody?" (*The Golden Gate* 3)

Neither does John understand nor does he admit that he desperately needs being put into frame of relationships which others are shown enjoying. They are represented by friends (Jan, Phil, Ed), loving companions (Liz, Jan), family members (Chuck, Paul, John Jr.), mother-child (Mrs. Dorati and Her Children). Even pets convey bonds which are shown throughout. Finally, all find a refuge in Phil's home. This is so because Phil believed in family right from the beginning. On the other hand, John ridicules Jan for giving the advertisement, then he laughs at the marriage-materials and the family-types. As a result of this, he is seen forlorn and haunted in absence of Jan (She represented the feelings of relationship, bonds and togetherness). He suffers from the lack of belongingness, a feeling to be missed by somebody when you die. John realizes that 'life discovers purpose through companionship' (47).

So the novel uncovers the real-life-feel which is hidden in the layers of love and belongingness. Cancelling these bonds is the outlook of a materialistic generation, who finally lands up in utter confusion. Success doesn't help their frustration and status can't handle their depression. John's mother has died and father is unconcerned, so he is suffering from acute loneliness;

> John feels a cold cast of self pity
> Envelop him, no family
> Cushions his solitude further
> A linkless node, no spouse or sibling
> No children. John wonders alone. (*The Golden Gate* 6)

Agonised, he turns to Janet, who is his former love also. They had broken up as commitment suffocated John. Janet diagnoses that he badly needs a lover. Janet helps him to find a companion, Elizabeth—a Law student, through newspaper advertisement. John and Liz get along comfortably but Liz's binding to her pet turns into rejection from John. Almost on the verge of marriage Liz and John break up because John is intolerant towards Liz's earlier bonds. Obviously, misunderstandings arise and their relationship fails because John fails to recognise value of space in bonds. So John is back to square one. He avoids Janet due to embarrassment, but she discovers him suffering alone and moves forward to hold his hand. She doesn't allow him to be a self-destroying loner. This time Janet takes complete charge of John and they gradually become sole-mates. They have discovered seeds of mutual companionship. Unfortunately for John, Janet dies in a car accident and leaves John completely shattered as Liz has already married Phil but Janet's bond with John has not been in vain. The last sonnet shows her as an assurance and solace for

John even after she dies. She is clearly seen, even in her absence, directing him towards a purpose that we call life. Here Seth reminds of John Donne when he treats love on metaphysical plane.

Phil and Claire (another pair) make typical example of modern hollow relationships. They had a love marriage against the will of Claire's family. They lived happily for six years, had a son, purchased a piano, plenty of furniture, a Ford Capri, insurance, dish washer, T.V. set and a few others of the kind. In the midst of unromantic chores of household, Claire's family convinced her that Phil was dominating her and their ways fell apart. This results into an exclusive binding between Phil and Paul (father-son) who are introduced almost mourning at the 'burial of their bond' with Claire. Now centre of Phil's world is Paul and Paul is the motivational force in his father's life. Contrasted with Phil is presented the protagonist John, for whom life is a futile exercise and he wanders in the wilderness of world in search of belongingness. It hurts that only he is alone. A new combination is created and that is—Phil and Liz. Liz married Phil when John shockingly deserted her. In the background is Liz's mother who is fast approaching towards death. She desperately wants, at least one of her three children, to be settled in marriage. Liz who had earlier run away from an arranged marriage, is now unable to think about anything else, accept for whatever she can give to her dying mother as a gesture of thanks for a life-time of love and understanding. Also, she clearly understands that her own judgement was not sound enough to prove it. Phil is already suffering a broken marriage, but holds on tightly to the string that binds him to his son Paul. Liz now wants stability in life, so in a similar state of mind they marry and their home accommodates Janet's pet as Janet has died, Dr. Matt's son as the couple have also died in the accident. Apart from the love and reminiscence of Liz's dying mother, the short-lived bond between Liz and John has also been duly honoured, as they name their newly born after John.

Liz's mother Marie Dorati and Mr. Dorati are another pair who have cherished a long married company. Even in old age,

Mr. Dorati's world has beauty and meanings only if Mrs. Dorati is a part of it. Again Mrs. Dorati and her son Ed represent a beautiful and powerful mother-son bond. Ed tries his best to become a good human being, as he cares a lot about the values his mother and family gave him. Though morality constantly remains a point in consideration, Ed's concern, in discussing morality, is based on honouring his bonds with his family and society. No doubt that man-woman relationship begins with the account of a break-up between Phil and Claire but story ends with a happy home of Liz on the pattern of Mr. and Mrs. Dorati.

Another theme that runs parallel is nuclear warfare, which is also a result of material race of America. Hallowman of materially successful America, is frustrated and self-destructive. This tendency for frustration has brought about the game of nuclear warfare. Still, major theme of the novel is the universal undercurrent of life: man's search for love. He also traces various challenges that human beings face during this search. The story-line, set in California, is about a relatively advanced patch of society. Obviously, it seems ahead of times for Indian imagination. No wonder, love is the raw material that has been used to shape these bonds. It also highlights the basic strength of love, which lies in the give and take theory. However, it has different meanings for different characters. Whereas nothing substantial for John, it is sadder but wiser for Phil and Liz, for Ed it is honouring his surroundings and creator. By and large, it is a comfortable sharing of responsibilities, respect, loyalty and belongingness.

A Suitable Boy which created buzz in the corridors of international honours and prize ceremonies, is a mega narrative of three generations and their surroundings of post-independence India. After *The Golden Gate* in California, it was author's intellectually coming home as he is finally merged with the social, political, religious trends of the time, from one end of the country to the other. Apart from other contemporary issues: marriage, family, home—all provide a running structure. Mrs. Rupa Mehra has to find a suitable match for her rather unconventional daughter Lata. Mrs. Rupa Mehra is one who has lost a home, shares a home, and wants to create and possess a home. So in these various considerations 'home' proves to be an object of prime importance. Finally, the puzzle is solved and the suitable boy is one who provides you with physical and emotional assurance—suggested by home. Like Bernard Shaw's choice of Morell in 'Candida' and Bluntschli in 'Arms and the Man', Rupa Mehra's stand proves wisdom on a practical scale.

The novel begins in a tone, ridiculing the conventional celebration of marriage but passing through a long scrutiny, it ends at a cool-headed decision, like in *The Golden Gate* in favour of stability of bonds—through marriage. Lata is the protagonist who doesn't believe in traditional concept and form of marriage. Therefore, she finds the arranged marriage of her elder sister monotonous and, to some extent, non-engaging. She enjoys falling in love with Kabir—a Muslim boy and justifies her claim to take her own decisions. Moreover, temperamentally she is not the typical self-sacrificing Indian daughter. Still in the end she decides to marry a clear-headed, practical-minded Haresh who happens to be her Mother's choice. An important factor along with others, in rejecting Kabir, is the fact that her mother is unable to accept Kabir. So marrying Haresh, keeps the bond between mother and daughter almost undisturbed. Lata concludes on wisdom that she derives out of this analysis. Now she can decipher love which is an illusion in absence of mutual binding. Marriage, to her, is clarity which leads to a purposefulness. Seth brings home the value of binding in relationships: "All I meant was that when I am with Kabir, or even away from him but thinking about him, I become utterly useless for anything. I feel I am out of control—like a boat heading for the rocks—and I don't want to become a wreck" (1198), so clearly and emphatically Seth establishes the value of the institution leading to fruitful bonds. A contrasted set of characters is Arun (Lata's brother) and Meenakshi (Arun's wife). Bond, in this marriage, is almost non-existent. Absence of mutual faith and respect in this marriage, leads to a final ruin of family and individuals. Having fallen in love, at a point of time, doesn't come to save their marital bonds.

Again, Prof. Pran Kapoor and Savita (Lata's sister) have gone for an arranged marriage. They gradually develop a fondness which binds them to each other and so they pass through the twists and turns of life in an assured manner. Mrs. Rupa Mehra's multifaceted bonds serve as a general structure of society, which has been portrayed throughout the novel. Extended family, personal friends, family friends—all supply with a material of relationships that makes 'A Suitable Boy' intricate and intimate at the same time. There seems to be a question running as an undercurrent through the juxtaposition of the arranged marriage of Savita-Pran and love marriage of Arun-Meenakshi. The marriages may break but the bonds are forever. There's no denying the fact that they are strained from time to time but their spirit is mighty enough to go through any kind of trial. To save her parallel bonds from strain, Lata chooses the self-effacing cobbler as compared to the dashing young cricketer or the poet-novelist. Though non-glamourous, he proves quite capable of creating and conveying a sense of responsibility towards the home and affection towards assurance in relationship. So also, personality formation of certain characters shows an important role, played there, by mutual bonds. Kabir can't afford to cancel his disturbed past and parentage. Maan Kapoor, though a free mind and soul, can't walk out of the close-knit boundaries of family relationships, not even for his obsessive love for Saeeda Begum. Even the core politician Mahesh Kapoor's personal constitution is based on and supported by the powerful nerves of family and friendship. Surrounded by misunderstandings outside, Mahesh Kapoor shares his worries with his wife, even if she is not capable of understanding the complication of politics. Her presence in Mahesh Kapoor's life serves as a relief in time of crisis. Even in a rapidly rotting political scenerio, realpolitic, manipulation, napotism and communalism have not been able to erode the bonds between Maan Kapoor and Saeeda, Mann and his friends, Mahesh Kapoor and his wife etc. In short, walking through a mess of mechanising relationships, Seth tries to hold a torch of purity and simplicity which helps us to understand what is more important today—admiration and celebration of the blessings of a simple life or giving your life to understanding baseless complexities and complications of present day? By all means, to make life simple is worth celebration and establishing this fact is really important.

Two Lives, which is biography and memoir at once, is a narrative of celebration of a love-affair, creating bonds across social and geographical divide. With the Second World War serving as background, the book spontaneously proves to be dealing with the theme of love and war. However, gradually love and binding takes the centre stage. This can be taken as an account of bonds identified, nourished and celebrated by two hearts, who never fell in love at first sight. But once the bonds developed, there was nothing that could disturb the feel. Shanti (an Indian) uncle of author's mother, goes to Germany (before independence) to study dentistry. When considered as a lodger by Henny's family, her first reaction to her future companion was, 'Don't take the black man'. But gradually a mutual liking grew up. They became good friends.

Chance has its strange ways to direct the course of human life. When Henny fled to Hitler's Germany she was received by no other person than Shanti at Victoria Station. He was the only one she knew in that 'Unknown land'. They lived a life of togetherness, shared each others' pains and pleasures and married later. Shanti, who had lost his right arm in the battle of Monte Cassino, set up in his profession with a rare courage to defy his injury. Henny had virtually become his right hand. They were a couple with different opinions which they mutually respected, for example, Henny never visited India and, that too, on the pretext that she didn't like the place. Intimacy of their bonds was not to be affected by the individual difference. Shanti's profession had new meanings as Henny helped him to perform the operations as a dentist. As it goes in Hindu mythology that a man is complete only after the other half joins through intimacy of bonds, so their mutual commitment, through bonds, made them complementary to each other. The book opens with a boy of seventeen (the author) reaching the home of his mother's uncle Shanti, in England. This boy had met them once earlier, when he was a small child, but nothing was fresh in his memory now. They were going to be his guardians in England, where he had gone to study. Though the fact remains that uncle Shanti has not been in regular touch with his family in India, still this young boy's staying with them, during his impressionable years, leaves him fond of them. He finds them quite inspiring and feels like knowing more and more about them. So much so, that a son in him wants to save his great uncle Shanti and Henny from vanishing in oblivion. The 'Dedication' of the *Two Lives* records:

> Does this half-filial endeavour
> Hold half a chance of half-success—
> Even to track your lives, much less
> Not to let thee recede for ever?
> No, if I'd hoped to grasp the whole;
> Yes, if some shard may touch the soul.

No doubt the book starts with a sharp contrast of East and West, a young boy of seventeen is exposed to anything and everything of complicated modern European society. But in the end this boy essentially comes home when we see that his magnum opus *A Suitable Boy* dedicated to his maternal grandmother, rests on the relevance of bonds. *Two Lives* closes with a note of much valued love that this couple showered on their great nephew. Home is treated as an essential feature that enfolds people, incidents, attitudes of a century and finally this boy (author) visits the same place—18, Queens Road, Hendon to close the book. Seth himself calls it a son-like homage to his forefathers. What influences him deeply is that the main consideration in Henny's marrying Shanti, has been his respect for her pain and suffering over the loss of her parents during Hitler's operations. The book contains a number of personal letters which suggest the meaningful bindings in the couple's life. Shanti writes his first letter to Henny after his injury in the Second World War:

> Dear Hennerle
> Most aweful thing has happened to me, my right forearm was completely severed by a shell.... (56)

He closes another letter on:

> Yours in pain but in love. (159)

This belongingness had worked as undefeated life-force for Shanti and Henny in a foreign land.

In this way, we have relationship, family, bonds and home which give a framework to this grand love story. *Two lives* assumes a special meaning and value as it must have been tough job to establish love in the background of the worst wars of modern civilization. World wars in themselves, are an evidence that man has stopped honouring his bond with self and with humanness. In a mood, when we are denying the force of man's bonding with his internal world, it is not easy to discover love in the hearts, already disillusioned by war and deromanticized by their advancing age. They discover the power of love, at a turn of age, when we are finally disillusioned and fed-up with the stupidity of commonly known notion of love. No doubt, presenting a combination of forces working within and outside human heart and mind, is wonderful in terms of its valuable message. Our modern world is acutely suffering from the absence of love. Resultantly hatred, by and large, is continuously ailing the health of modern civilization.

All said and done, it is a well-established fact that the literary world of Vikram Seth is essentially a world of human bonds. A giant of modern literary world, like Seth, has by all means, done a valuable service to this 'Waste Land' by presenting the power and value of universal human bonds in a modern package. His works are known for a masterly style which displays Seth's luxurious sporting with language. Technique and presentation of *A Suitable Boy* has been enjoyed and admired not only by the readers but also by those who are already in the field of writing. *The Golden Gate* is a specimen of his spontaneous flow from one sonnet to the other. Flowing narrative leaves us with a literary delicacy, known as poetic fiction. Sonnets seem to be his all-time favourite as his prose fictional works also have dedication and contents expressed in sonnets. Though he is known for experimenting with alternate ideas on morality, institutions and such things, but at the same time, he doesn't forget his duty as a writer. He examines the traditional value-system, offers free debates on issues like live-in-relationship, alternate sexuality, relevance of marriage, and then tries to show the essence and spirit of the subject. He mocks at hypocrisy of Mrs. Rupa Mehra in *A Suitable Boy* when she is after finding a suitable match by all means. But, no disrespect is meant. He doesn't believe in carrying the load of waste in relationships because he doesn't hesitate in calling a spade—a spade. It is shocking to know that Phil and Claire's broken marriage is a solace to her aunts just because they were not consulted while making a decision.

Seth analyses age-old values as they need to go through a revision, and carefully holds the beauty of relevant features. Not only through his characters, he himself strongly supports the wisdom and useful aspects of our traditional set-up. Through this revision he has done a neat job to remove suffocation from age-old notions. Unfortunately, due to suffocation, present generation has started cancelling or avoiding traditional values. In the name of a transparent society, they have started showcasing blemishes. Seth's analysis comes as a help at such a time. Presenting a universal value in a fashionable statement, helps him to transcend time and place. He reminds of Wordsworth's 'type of wise who soar but never roam' in *To The Skylark* (Wordsworth *The Skylark*). The more the bird contemplates on his home, the more vigorous becomes his song. Indian philosophy is peculiarly based on the concept of a purposeful life. In agreement with this T.S. Eliot ends his poem *The Waste Land* at Indian scene and Upnishadic closing. Seth has perhaps realized this fact, and has created an undercurrent of bonds and relationships which must lead us to a life, based on action supporting a purpose. Course of action in life of all the characters is governed by their sense of belonging to someone special in their life. Someone who loves them and as a response to this love, they wish to do something for him. All major decisions of their life are influenced by these bonds. In short, binding—real and sometimes even superficial, works towards making life meaningful. Seth has, through an immense variety, defined different bonds on the basis of their relevance. Bonds create understanding, give a purpose, work as a driving force, help us fight against odds, and, above all, keep us in a normal mind-frame. He has also followed frail and short-distance bonds, that are incapable of enduring pressure. The writer honours even these short-lived relationships. Once dead, they are given a proper burial (Lata and Kabir, Arun and Minakshi) by the author. In short, his writings seem to be an intense effort to understand the baffling variety of strings that bind human-beings to one another. He establishes the fact that families and homes are indispensable. This world may become a strange place with spider and lizard (iguana) as pets, but basic needs of man's inner world will always be the same.

Today's multi-tasking generation is bewildered and confused with a denial of self, but, Vikram Seth seems to be continuously celebrating the return of the prodigal son which is supported by his statement: "I have always felt like the son in some ways. I think that's true of all extended families, as true of Italian or Jewish families as Indian ones. You never gain independence. In your imagination, you are always someone's child, long dead though they may be" [Interview with Tim Adams]. Sense of belonging is still as charming as ever, and Vikram Seth is one writer who doesn't appreciate hiding this natural beauty of human heart. That's why we always find bonds, scattered as raw material, and Vikram Seth designs his choicest literary models with *Bonds*—that are spontaneously identified, nourished and preserved bonds—that have an inbuilt power to travel across historical and geographical boundaries.

WORKS CITED

Eliot, T.S. *Poetic Works*. London: Oxford University Press, 1975.

"Interview with Tim Adams." *The Hindu*, Sep. 25, 2005.

Seth, Vikram. *The Golden Gate*. New Delhi: Penguin Books, 1986.

——. *A Suitable Boy*. New Delhi: Penguin Books, 1993.

——. *Two Lives*. New Delhi: Penguin Books, 2005.

Wordsworth, William. *Poetic Works*, London.

The Psyche of Crisis: A Creative Impulse in the Poetry of A.K. Ramanujan

21

Neeta

In the wake of globalisation, community of Indian diaspora is increasing fast and it is gaining distinctive identity in world literature. Indians constitute one of the largest immigrant groups, having a sizeable population. People usually migrate from their homeland to some alien one for their intellectual and material well-being. But this geographical and physical displacement often do not coincide with their cultural and psychological one. In spite of living at the land of their adoption, they have a tendency to look across time and space to their native land. Their existence on the alien land makes them feel displaced, marginalised and culturally segregated in the midst of the confrontation of values at social, cultural, religious and moral levels. Both the value systems—of the native land and of the adopted one, have their own claim to pull them and in such conditions they begin to suffer from a psychic crisis. On the one hand, they feel nostalgic and long for their home and on the other, they try to move from margins to the centre and wish to assimilate in the culture of alien land. To the writers and men of letters, the exile proves to be a source of creation. Through their art, they reshape and also revive their memories. Terry Eagleton observes that the exile is productive for the writers. The exile's approach to society containing what he terms "tensions" ("remembered" and "real", "integrations and "dispossession") make for great art. To mitigate their desire to go back to the roots, they often make imaginary homelands from the fragmentary memories of their native land, as it has been pointed out by Salman Rushdie:

> It may be that when the Indian writer who writes from outside India tries to reflect that world, he is obliged to deal in broken mirrors, some of whose fragments have been irretrievably lost...but these fragmentations made trivial things seem like symbols and then mundane acquired numinous qualities. (Qtd by Shrotiya 37)

A.K. Ramanujan is one of those artists whose creative sensibility has been moulded under the pressure of two diverse socio-cultural identities. He was born and brought up in Mysore (South India). After finishing his education from Mysore University, he worked as a scholar and a lecturer at different educational institutes and universities in India and subsequently shifted to USA as a Professor of Linguistics and South Asian Languages and Civilization at the University of Chicago and stayed there till the end of his life. In this shift of location, his sensibility shared the counter influences of Indian and Western cultural traditions. It paved a way for all the pervasive diasporic sensibility, reflected in his poetic creed. His poetry contains all the distinctive attributes of cross-cultural crisis. Despite of sharing a number of qualities of Indian diaspora like nostalgia, homelessness, identity crisis etc., his vision is different from others in the respect that the confrontation of the values of the East and the West does not mar his sensibility negatively rather it provided a refreshing impetus to his creativity. In the words of a reviewer: "While he is searching for roots in an alien idiom, he achieves a synthesis which results in enhancement of both his vision and language" (Chellappan and Bhashyam 96). His Indian past and American present are not the two separate factors affecting his sensibility rather they are complementary to each other. He himself asserts in one of his essays "Is there an Indian way of thinking?" that the Eastern and the Western are like the two lobes of brain and they can co-exist. Appreciating this marvelous quality of Ramanujan, a reviewer writes:

> Ramanujan is unique in his ability to contain within himself the binaries, explaining the East to the West and the West to the East with perfect equanimity. (Ramakrishna 11)

It means that the value system of both the lands—native and alien, co-ordinates in making him a superb artist. Though at the psychological level, he also suffers like other members of diasporic community and longs for his memorable past yet it does not hinder his creativity. His native culture of past, after confrontation with the alien present, always provides a new and enlightening meaning of life. In one of his interviews, he reveals the fact:

> The past never passes, either the individual past or historical past or cultural past. It is with us....the disconnection is as much an understanding of the past as making the connection. And the living in the present have to see both. (Interview 78)

The present paper is an attempt to evaluate Ramanujan's poetry with a view to establish that in spite of sharing the characteristics of diasporic writers, he is unique in his capability to turn his psychic crisis into a beautiful world of poetic creation.

'Family' is the central metaphor, standing for 'society' at large in the poetry of A.K. Ramanujan (Shinde 103). In almost all the volumes of his poems, he has composed poems related to the theme of family and familial relationships. His Brahminic heritage from a reputed South Indian family inculcates a desire in him to have a joint family with a host of relationships under one roof, though the Western culture approaches him with the concept of nuclear family having husband, wife and children only. His poems like *Extended Family* and *Small-Scale Reflection on a Great House* are the outcome of his longing for Indian joint family. In his nostalgic mood, he compares himself to the different members of a joint family—like his "grandfather" he bathes "before the village crow", slaps "Soap on my back/ like father", hears "faint morning song like "mother", "play garden/ in and out/ the bath tub" like his "grandson". With his concept of *Vasudev Kutumbkam*, he longs for generations living under one roof, making each other's sense of belonging stronger. Such families have superb power of absorption and can easily subside the weaknesses and handicaps of each of its members:

> Things come in everyday
> to lose themselves among other things
> lost long ago among
> other things lost long ago. (96)

Individualism is not the keynote of such families rather the common interests are taken into consideration by each member and in a way, save them from being the victims of "rootlessness", while as in the nuclear family with its independent status in the society freedom is given to its members for the utmost development of 'self' but it has its own pitfalls:

> The nuclear family, which is essentially 'urban' in nature, tends to be a mobile one, physically and socially, and it, therefore, tends towards a certain rootlessness. The sense of 'belonging' born in living together for generations, which is a characteristic feature of an extended family, is absent or weak in nuclear family. (Shinde 112)

Whenever Ramanujan looks at his own nuclear family in America, he is reminded of the joint family culture of India that is why in a number of poems, he seems to yearn for various familial relationships like in *Of Mothers, Among Other Things*, he tells about his deep attachment for mother, in *A Leaky Tap After a Sister's Wedding*, he describes sister's "high swing". *Looking for a Cousin on a Swing* reveals his experiences with his cousin on a swing, in *Saturday* he revives in his memory his "brother's briar pipe". Thus, by reviving these memories, he wants to re-live them through his imagination so that he may feel at ease in the existing situations as the same has also been observed by M.K. Naik:

> It is not emotion recollected in tranquility but recollection emotionalised in untranquail moments that appears to be driving force behind much of Ramanujan's poetry. (15)

Husband-wife relationship is a pivot for strong familial ties. Ramanujan's Hindu heritage and the Western culture, brought to him by his Syrian Christian wife, often clash in this regard. He has composed a series of poems related to his dilemma, in understanding the true nature of this tender relationship. His deep roots in Indian tradition often lay hindrances in his adjustment with his Syrian Christian wife in an alien land. Whenever, he thinks seriously about his relations with his wife, the role models which appear before his eyes are his parents. The mother is merely the symbol of "sacrifice" while the image of father signifies "power". Though he wants to inculcate certain changes in his personality, according to the changed milieu, his relations with his wife could not remain cordial because the cultural differences in their ideologies often become hostile to their happy union. His first poem in the Love series "Love! What She Said", reveals an ideal wife according to his Hindu concept. She is one who used to love and respect her husband in spite of several weaknesses in him:

> His face is rajor lean.
> His liver is on hold.
> He raped his niece.
> She's dead.
> ....
> Yet I grow lean.
> His heart is gold
> to my greed. My eyes
> are fed.
> When he turns his head. (219)

But just in another poem "Love Poem for a Wife 2" he expresses the helplessness of an Indian who is trying to adjust and readjust his behavioural patterns to make his married life meaningful, but ultimately feels at a loss:

> I dreamed one day
> that face my own yet hers,
> with my own nowhere
> to be found; lost; cut
> loose like my dragnet
> past. (84)

Ramanujan, of course, felt disturbed by such a crisis throughout his life, yet his creative impulse does not get affected by it. While searching for the possible causes about this unharmonious relationship, he finds in "Love Poem for a Wife 1" that their "unshared childhood" is responsible for it. The solution he also provides is that either the patterns of "Egyptian" should be followed, where "their king had sisters for queens to continue incest/ of childhood into marriage" or the Hindu religion should be followed:

> betroth us before birth,
> forestalling separate horoscopes
> and mothers' first periods,
> and wed us in the oral cradle
> and carry marriage back into
> the namelessness of childhoods. (67)

Ultimately, the crisis which initiated with his living in an alien milieu gets resolved in his Hindu heritage. He weaves the web of family relations through his poetic imagination and makes efforts to enjoy the bliss of family life by using the images of Indian contexts of family.

A.K. Ramanujan's Hindu consciousness remains a central motif in his poems related to religion. He is often confronted with a cleavage between Eastern and Western religious values as it can be appreciated in the poem *Waterfalls in a Bank*:

> As I transact with the past as with another
> country with its own customs, currency,
> stock exchange, always
> at a loss when I count my change: (189)

But to overcome these perplexing situations, he begins to interpret his inherent value system with reference to his changed milieu. In spite of knowing the exact meaning of modernity, he ultimately declares:

> I cannot unlearn
> Conventions of despair.
> They have their pride.
> I must seek and will find
> my particular hell in my Hindu mind. (34)

He can even refuse to possess the "second sight", which a Hindu usually pretends to possess and he describes his pitiable condition when he is asked about this possession by a foreigner:

I fumble in my nine
Pockets like the night blind
Son-in-law groping
in every room for his wife,
and strike a light to regain
at once my first, and only sight. (191)

This confession of his inability to stick to his roots indicates that he does not want to bear the tearing tension of cross-cultural currents rather he wants to take one sided decision to accept or reject a particular value. As he is a learned man with deep understanding, he evolves his own value system whenever he passes through the turmoil of confrontation. His poem "A Hindu to His Body" deals with the theme of the place of "Body" in human life. In the poem he seems to accept some of the Indian and a few of the Western points of view. The poem begins with his approval of Western ideology when he calls body as "Dear Pursuing Presence", because Hindu view does not regard "body" as "dear", something to be pursued. The ultimate objective of life, according to Hindu religion, is to get *moksha,* i.e. the permanent liberation of soul from the bondages of body and its ultimate mystification with *Brahma.* But in the concluding part of the poem, the poet like a true follower of Hindu religion, wishes for unity of all life, i.e. human, animal and vegetable. In the following lines, he expresses his intense desire:

to rise in the sap of trees
let me go with you and feel the weight
of honey-lives in my branching
and the burlap weave of the weaver-birds in my hair. (40)

Here he seems to reject the Western ideology which maintains dichotomy between man and nature and also man and lower animal. Similarly, his poem "The Death and the Good Citizen", expresses his independent judgement, unaffected by both philosophies—The East and the West. After his death he neither wants to be cremated in a Western manner by lying out "in a funeral parlour" embalmed by 'pesticides' nor is he satisfied with the Indian manner of cremation in "Sanskrit and sandalwood." In the concluding part of the poem, he expresses his own liberal idea, regarding the way of cremation in which he wishes to be the part of nature after his death:

> My tissue will never graft,
> will never know newsprint
> never grow in a culture
> or be mould and compost
> for jasmine egg plant
> and the unearthly perfection
> of municipal oranges. (136)

His famous Hindu poems too, stand in true testimony of his rational outlook. The poem "The Hindoo: the only Risk" points out how the ideal of *Sthitaprajna* is degenerated to indifference. "The Hindoo: He doesn't Hurt a Fly or a Spider either" reveals how the great Hindu principle of non-violence degenerates into cowardice: "It's time I told you why/ I'm so gentle, do not hurt a fly." Thus, in spite of feeling proud of his Hindu heritage, he can easily find weaknesses in it and be satiric towards some of its values. His motive is not to reject the traditional knowledge rather he reinscribes and gives new and fresh meanings to it.

In spite of being rational in taking decision to accept or reject particular values from the East and the West, he is sometimes caught in the net of confusion. His poem "Still Another View of Grace" reveals how the persona, proud of his cultural heritage, "Bred Brahmin among the Singers of Shivering Hymns", ultimately succumbs to the lustful desires:

> .... Commandments crumbled
> in my father's past, her tumbled hair suddenly known
> as silk in my angry hand, I shook a little
> and took her, behind the laws of my land. (45)

Whole of the poem shows the efforts of persona to check himself from becoming the victim of the lustful desires but the last stanza reflects the forcefulness of the changed environment which ultimately leads to the degradation of morals according to his Hindu heritage. In the words of S.N. Pandey:

> "Conventions of Despair" begins in the midst of an argument which has engaged the poet's persona for a

> quite sometime. There seems to have been an upsetting tussle in the poet's psyche between the values of modernism and those asceticism each trying to get the better of other. [Pandey Introduction]

Under such conditions he often feels dejected, realising: "Connection severed.../ I lose my bearings" (185) and sometimes, aspires to revive his connection with his cultural past, "Connect! Connect! cries my disconnecting/ madness, remembering phrases" (178). These longings for connection make it clear that the acceptance of some of the Western values could never blot out his glorious Indian past from his memory. In one of his collected essays, he himself asserted the fact: "In a culture like the Indian, the past does not pass. It keeps on providing paradigms and ironies for the present" (187).

Not only the Indian values and morals are re-oriented or re-organised by his rational sensibility but the values of the West are also scrutinized by it. Living at the land of glamour, he did not confine his vision to the surface only rather he peeps into it to evaluate it from the eyes of an easterner. His poem "Take Care" stands in true testimony of it, where he faithfully describes the unsatisfactory life of modern cities like Chicago. It is the city of extremes where "it blows hot and cold", i.e. life here is, never balanced or normal. Defining its characteristics in a sarcastic manner, he says here "Friends have doubts" and "wives had lawyers" which is quite opposite to the Indian morals of 'friendship' and 'wifehood'. Throughout the poem, he has pointed out the details of the artificially mannered and imposed kind of Western lifestyle which is in sharp contrast to simple and natural lifestyle of the East. In Chicago people live in tall buildings, drawing the "blinds" on their "windows" i.e. maintain privacy in place of sociability, "daughters" get 'pills' and "learn Karate" for fear of getting "raped", i.e. decency is not the part of this society. People here suffer from a sense of fear as the bomb may be "in the barber's chair" or "the knife/ on the museum stair." Seeing such condition of society and people living here, he warns the Easterners:

> In Chicago
> do not walk slow

Find no time
to stand and stare
Down there, blacks look black
And whites, they look blacker. (104)

Ramanujan's diasporic sensibility is also reflected in his physic crisis between the rapidly growing knowledge of science and often forgotten knowledge of traditional Indian values. But even out of this crisis he can beautifully weave a poem "Pain". Here the persona seems to have revive his faith in the dictum 'ignorance is bliss'. Wherever someone consults a doctor for the treatment of some disease, a number of investigations are made on the sufferer. Enormous amount of gathered knowledge by the scientists make the case more critical and the diseased begins to feel much disturbed at the psychological level. In such conditions, our traditional knowledge appears to be more beneficial than the modern one:

O god of knowledge, busy wizard
of diagnosis, father of needles, dials,
and test tubes, send your old companion here,
that mother of mothers, goddess though of ignorance
send her soon so she can kiss away my pain
as she has always done. (274)

Here the poet wants to make the point clear that increasing scientific knowledge has further intensified the crisis of man, rather than solving it. His loss of 'faith' resulted into his weak anchorage on life as a whole. Midst this loss of faith, the persona often suffers from the loss of identity as Ramanujan beautifully presents in his short poem "Self-portrait":

I resemble everyone
but myself, and sometimes see
in shop-windows
despite the well known laws
of optics,
the portrait of a stranger,
date unknown,
often signed in a corner
by my father. (23)

Even in this poem, the poet metaphorically represents the loss of traditional values by the loss of image in the mirror. While signature of the father in the corner indicates that the traditional values cannot be easily blotted out so it is not good on our part to make efforts to forget them rather it would be better for us to learn the art of adjustment with these memories.

A.K. Ramanujan is a genius, who very skilfully converts his psychic crisis into beautiful gems of poetic creation. The confrontation of values related to the different spheres of life like family and familial relationship, religion, morality, science etc. has often been reconciled by his rational outlook. Evaluating and critically analysing the contradictory pulls from the divergent cultures, he comes to draw an amenable solution which not only keeps him in touch with the land of his origin but also helps him in assimilating with the socio-cultural milieu of the land of his domicile. He, like a firm tree, never gets uprooted in the midst of the cross-cultural torrents from the East and the West. His roots often get sustenance from his Indian past and the blossoms often appear in the West, having colours of the perfect symbiosis of both the Eastern and the Western ethos. Niranjan Mohanty appreciates him in one of his articles:

> Ramanujan's poetry should not be assumed to have originated from the Hindu or Indian milieu, should rather be seen from the perspective of the symbiosis of the "outer" and "inner" substances. (117)

So A.K. Ramanujan's rootedness in Indian culture and involvement with American culture has resulted in his skilful articulation of both the Indian and Western ideas with ease.

WORKS CITED

Chellappan, K. and Kanaka Bhashyam. "Encounter and Synthesis in the Poetry of A.K. Ramanujan." *Journal of Indian Writing in English.* Vol. XII No. 2, 1984.

Dharwadkar, Vinay. Ed. *The Collected Poems of A.K. Ramanujan.* New Delhi: Oxford University Press, 2003. (All references made in the paper are from this collection.)

——. *The Collected Essays of A.K. Ramanujan.* New Delhi: Oxford University Press, 2003.

Jha, Rama. "A Conversation with A.K. Ramanujan." *Humanities Press*, Vol. III, No. 1.

Mohanty, Niranjan. "Things as They Are: Poetry of A.K. Ramanujan." *Journal of South Asian Literature*, Spring-Fall, 1993.

Naik, M.K. "A.K. Ramanujan's Search for Roots." *Dimensions of Indian English Literature*. New Delhi: Sterling Publishers, 1984.

Pandey, S.N. "Introduction: The Axis of Ramanujan's Cultural Preoccupations." *Millennium Perspectives on A.K. Ramanujan*. New Delhi: Atlantic Publishers and Distributors Pvt. Ltd., 2001.

Ramakrishna, C.D. "Ramanujan's Credo." *Millennium Perspectives on A.K. Ramanujan*. Ed. Surya Nath Pandey. New Delhi: Atlantic Publishers and Distributors Pvt. Ltd., 2001.

Shinde, Jaya Prakash A. "Family as a Central Metaphor in A.K. Ramanujan's Poetry." *Millennium Perspectives on A.K. Ramanujan*. Ed. Surya Nath Pandey. New Delhi: Atlantic Publishers and Distributors Pvt. Ltd., 2001.

Shrotiya, Niru A. "Images in the Broken Mirror: Narrative Techniques in Salman Rushdie's *Midnight's Children.*" *Perspectives on Indian English Fiction*. Ed. Jaydipsinh Dodiya. New Delhi: Dormant Publishers, 2002.

Uma Parameswaran's *The Door I Shut Behind Me*: A Diasporic Text

22

Anuradha Verma

Diaspora is an emerging word in literature. It means "the dispersion of people from their traditional homeland."

According to *William Safran,* the term diaspora can be "applied to expatriate minority communities whose members shall share several of the following characteristics they retain: a collective memory, vision or myth about their original homeland."

The literature of these diasporic communities is called *Diasporic Literature.* Today we have different diasporic literatures like the Indo-Canadian diasporic literature. The Indo-Canadian literature, as it is understood by the term itself, is the literature of those Indians who have migrated to Canada. It would be worth mentioning here that in 1971, Canada adopted a policy of "multiculturalism". It was officially adopted by the federal government of Canada. Canada is, thus, a multicultural country. Amidst this multicultural ethos, the East Indian diasporic writers are trying to establish their own identity. Many of the writers are concerned with describing the experiences of its ethnicity. Among the Indo-Canadian writers, the notables are *Uma Parameswaran, B. Rajan, Rohinton Mistry, Vassanji* etc.

Uma Parameswaran is one of the Indo-Canadian diasporic writers that includes immigrants of both sexes, of all ages from different professions and vocations, who like to adapt themselves in multicultural Canada.

Uma Parameswaran—a poet, playwright, short story writer and critic was born in Madras and grew up in Jabalpur, India.

Her father was a professor of Physics. She went to the college in Nagpur where she got a bachelor's and master's degree in English. She was a Fulbright Scholar, she received her MA in creative writing at Indiana University and a Ph.D. in English from Michigan State University in 1972. Living in Winnipeg since 1966, she is a professor of English at the University of Winnipeg. She is married to a mathematician and has one daughter.

She is the author and editor of several books of poetry, plays and criticism. She also won "1999 New Muse Award" and the *2000 Canadian Author's Association* "Jubilee Award" for her fiction—(Collection of Short Stories) *What was always Hers*. Uma Parameswaran is known for the contributions to the emerging field of South Asian Canadian Literature (SACLIT, the name coined by her).

Uma Parameswaran has devoted much of her efforts in the literary field to create an identifiable South Asian Canadian diaspora. For the past 25 years Uma has been actively involved in bringing Indian culture and heritage to the children of Winnipeg. In 1978, she organized the first formal dance training of its kind in Winnipeg. She founded PALI (Performing Arts and Literatures of India) for the purpose of introducing various aspects of Indian culture not only to the Indo-Canadian youth of Winnipeg but also to the community at large. She was the producer of her own weekly television show for over 10 years.

This story *The Door I Shut Behind Me* was written by Parameswaran in 1967. Parameswaran's stories contain the highest degree of cultural sensitivity. The present story is also a powerful work. By Parameswaran's writings, we are not only constantly aware of the South Asian experience but also of the struggle in life that makes us all human. Parameswaran has depicted a true picture of Indian Diaspora in Canada. She slowly explores the layers of self-doubt and anxiety that exist in the mind of an immigrant. Chander is the protagonist who arrives from India in Montreal, Canada. Kishen Agrawal and Harish Bahl are other characters who are lost in the affluence and cynosure of Canada and as well feel nostalgic for their homeland.

Chander was a very sophisticated, introvert man of 25 years. He had a Ph.D degree from Madras University. He was unmarried and had three brothers and two sisters. His partner who sat beside him in the plane was an unctuous man—Kishen Agrawal. He exuded friendliness and perfumed his hair. He was a foil of Chander as Chander was quiet, he was loud. Chander was reserved and shy, he was spontaneous in revealing his emotions. After landing on the soil of Canada, poor Chander had his company even in the hotel room. This man had only one-feeling that both belonged to the same country and were going to the same destination. It made him more friendly to Chander. This man Kishen Agrawal was a bundle of preconceptions and prejudices, a shallow, selfish and callow brute. Chander tolerated the droning of this man. When Agrawal glorified India—even Chander though sarcastically, gave the filthy picture of Indian society and Indian woman. This made Agrawal so disappointed that he started sobbing. The man till now who considered the Green Card as a magic wand, felt deep anguish for his homeland. He became nostalgic and spluttered:

> I am a Shopkeeper's son, my mother is a gossip and my wife is fat. My children do play on the street with snotty noses. But I love them. I want them. I would rather have them around me and me on my rope strung cot in my dung-polished courtyard than be this...here.... (141)

Chander envied Agrawal for his experience, his feeling of utter lostness, irrational onslaught of nostalgia for persons and a place. Chander had no yearning, no wonder at the sight and feel of a civilization so different from his own. Among diasporic community, a common problem is that of the language. We find this problem in Agrawal who said—

> I'd give anything in the world to see one of my own people to hear my own language. (142)

Chander realized that Agrawal was not talking of his family but of his linguistic community. But Chander wondered that whether it is only language that could hold a nation together. After hunting the Indian names from telephone directory,

Agrawal talked to Shrivastava who was going to Mundhras for an Indian get-together. Shrivastava proposed to pick them up and Agrawal accepted it. Agrawal was now very excited. He took betel packets with him in order to serve other Indians. After dinner, Mrs. Mundhra took them to a large living room where twenty odd persons were sitting. Chander, a shy man, could not mix up but soon Agrawal joined them, mixed with them. Chander was asked the same questions by everyone about his career and all of them gave assurances of their friendliness. Chander observed that Agrawal who recently was missing his linguistic community did not use native Hindi but talked in English. All of them spoke in English for people gathered belonged to different parts of India. Even children spoke very good English that Chander was ashamed of. He observed that the matured ones collected there for their ethnicity. They created an Indian ethos while their children even did not know anything about India—their religion and language. When Chander was asked about the condition of India he started by talking about drought, Indo-Chinese war, long queues everywhere for grain, fuel, milk, medicine. Soon he realised that nobody took actual interest in his description but sympathised him as if he was narrating some personal grief. When Chander spoke of the black-marketing, corruption and bribery, they remained unaffected by it. They were not at all bothered of the prevalent problems in India. Chander was very much hurt by their attitude. Giving no importance to this issue, one man changed the topic. Very soon once again conversation groups were formed. Chander was in Agrawal's group that was sorting out Agrawal's records. Chander was introspective. With increasing bewilderment, Chander observed their attitude. They enquired of Pankaj Mullick and Saigal's album. A young man enthusiastically, brandished the Saigal's record. There was a deep nostalgia in the air and Saigal's music in the background. Everyone talked of India. But the India they talked of was not the present India or the India when they left but the India during their boyhood times. Some remembered trams which trundled (ran) on Madras streets, some anti-British slogans, processions while some considered Lala Amarnath's century against Don

Bradman as the greatest event in cricket history. They romanticized their past tending to see no evil and brooking no negative views about their native country. They did not want to go back to India, not to experience those pleasures as was evident when Agrawal passed a plate of his betel, only few took packets. They no doubt reminisced about betel-areca shops, the roadside Romeos who gathered round the shop. Chander doubted their identification and said to himself in astonishment:

> What are they? Indians or Canadians? (145)

There people wanted to maintain their cultural ethos by meeting the people of same ethnicity on every Saturday of the month. They gathered to have just an ethnic get-together. They were not actually nostalgic or mesmerized by their native memories, but were having diasporic consciousness. Diasporic consciousness is a positive and celebrating linking across political borders of people who are of the same family. While living in Canada, they wanted to be close to their ethnicity by not changing their food habits and dressing.

This made Chander very confused, worried and eager. Their ambiguous condition is compared with *Trishanku*, a Hindu mythological king, suspended between two worlds. Chander learnt that these people were neither of *Here* nor of *Away* (India). One thing is vivid about immigrants that they never fully accepted either of the cultures and are suspended between two homes, two lives. This attitude made Chander grief-stricken. Now like Agrawal, he felt the streak of nostalgia which gave him great weight within himself. This weight gave him an inexplicable sense of loss, anger and contempt. Parameswaran in her paper *Dispelling the Spells of Memory* remarked that people who move from their native countries not only occupy but also bequeath to subsequent generations a 'liminality', an uneasy pull between two cultures. This pull was first felt by Agrawal and now by Chander. He sat quiet and still. Suddenly a pale, short man of thirty-six joined him. Chander was impressed by the ascetic bent of mind of this man whose name was Harish Bahl. But very soon the anguish emerged again when he learnt that this man married a Canadian woman. Chander hated the acceptance of Western culture.

The sense of exile became strong in him and he uttered with an anguish cry: "I don't expect here to be long and wanted to pick up some experience and go back home" (148).

This sense of rootlessness on this new land made him alienated. He had a strong urge to return to his homeland, when Bahl remarked that this is the usual cry of all the beginners and then they also contribute to the brain-drain casualty. Chander felt accused, he worries if he was abandoning India when she needs him most, if he is contributing to the brain-drain. Very soon we find that he comes out of the nostalgic-fever and becomes rational. He comes to the conclusion:

> This age is the age of individualism, and not of abstract ideologies of patriotism and nation-building. (148)

He feels a pull towards Canada. Near the end Harish declares:

> When we leave our country we shut many doors behind us though we are not aware of it at the time. (149) To this Chander responds, "There are many doors ahead of us". (149)

Thus, *The Door I Shut Behind Me* ends with a modern appeal for today that we are not only confined to our motherland but consider the entire globe as a single home.

Uma Parameswaran has thus delineated a wonderful picture of an immigrant experience. The message in the end is worth praising for it would be tough to find a character in today's literature, who thinks of Canada as an open door to the future. It reminds us of the lines said by Earle Birney:

> The centre is here and now the place on which we stand.

Contributors

A.N. Dwivedi. Formerly Professor, Department of English, Allahabad University, Allahabad, Uttar Pradesh.

Shrawan K. Sharma. Professor, Department of English, Gurukul Kangri University, Haridwar, Uttarakhand.

O.P. Budholia. Professor and Head, Department of English, Govt. K.R.G. Autonomous College, University of Jiwaji, Gwalior.

Beena Agarwal. Reader, Department of English, D.S. College, Aligarh, Uttar Pradesh.

Abha Shukla Kaushik. Reader, Department of English, A.K.P.G. College, Hapur, Ghaziabad, Uttar Pradesh.

Hemalatha K. Reader, Department of English, Kanya Gurukul Mahavidyalaya, Dehradun, Uttarakhand.

Ram Sharma. Senior Lecturer, Department of English, J.V. College, Baraut, Baghpat, Uttar Pradesh.

Archana Trivedi. Lecturer, Sir Chhotu Ram Institute of Engg. and Tech., C.C.S. University, Meerut, Uttar Pradesh

J.P. Savita. Formerly Reader and Head, Department of English, S.D. College, Muzaffarnagar, Uttar Pradesh.

Malti Agarwal. Reader and Head, Department of English, N.A.S. College, Meerut, Uttar Pradesh.

K.A. Agarwal. Formerly Reader, Department of English, Gurukul Kangri University, Haridwar, Uttarakhand.

Samina Khan. Reader, Department of English, Aligarh Muslim University, Aligarh, Uttar Pradesh.

Sangeeta Das. Reader, Department of English, D.G. College, Kanpur, Uttar Pradesh.

Shalini Gupta. Lecturer, Department of English, Khalsa College for Women, Sidhwan Khurd, Ludhiana, Punjab.

Satendra Kumar. Department of English, Govt. (P.G.) College, Lansedown, Uttarakhand.

Manoj Kumar. Department of English, Gurukul Kangri University, Haridwar, Urrarakhand.

T.S. Anand. Reader, Department of English, GGN Khalsa College, Ludhiana, Punjab.

Malti Sharma. Reader, Department of English, N.A.S. College, Meerut, Uttar Pradesh.

Neeta. Reader, Department of English, S.V. College, Aligarh, Uttar Pradesh.

Anuradha Verma. Research Scholar, N.A.S. (P.G.) College, Meerut, Uttar Pradesh.